Epistolophilia

Epistolophilia

Writing the Life of Ona Šimaitė

JULIJA ŠUKYS

University of Nebraska Press · Lincoln & London

© 2012 by Julija Šukys

The letters in chapters 4 and 11 appeared as "Letters from a Librarian: Lost and Found in Vilna." PMLA 118 (2003): 302–17.

Portions of the book, including parts of chapters 3 and 5, appeared in "Ona Šimaitė and the Vilnius Ghetto: An Unwritten Memoir." Lituanus 54 (2008): 5–25.

All rights reserved. Manufactured in the United States of America.

∞

Library of Congress Cataloging-in-Publication Data
Šukys, Julija. Epistolophilia: writing the life of Ona Šimaitė / Julija Šukys.   p. cm.
Includes bibliographical references.
ISBN 978-0-8032-3632-5 (cloth: alk. paper)

1. Šimaitė, Ona, 1894–1970. 2. Šimaitė, Ona, 1894–1970—Correspondence. 3. Šimaitė, Ona, 1894–1970—Diaries. 4. Biography—Authorship. 5. Righteous Gentiles in the Holocaust—Lithuania—Vilnius—Vilna—Biography. 6. Holocaust survivors—Lithuania—Vilnius—Vilna—Biography. 7. Holocaust, Jewish (1939–1945)—Lithuania—Vilnius—Vilna. 8. World War, 1939–1945—Jews—Rescue—Lithuania—Vilnius. 9. Librarians—Lithuania—Vilnius—Vilna—Biography. 10. Vilnius (Lithuania)—Biography. I. Title.
D804.66.S54S85 2012
940.53'18092—dc23
[B]   2011030426

FRONTISPIECE: Ona Šimaitė. F15-561. Mažvydas National Library of Lithuania Rare Books and Manuscripts Department.

Set in Arno by Kim Essman.
Designed by Nathan Putens.

*In memory of Ona
Šimaitė's friends:
Gershon Malakiewicz,
Kazys Jakubėnas,
Anna Abramowicz,
Tanya Shterntal,
and so many others.*

Epistolophilia /ɪ'pɪst(ə) lə(ʊ)'fɪlɪə/ *n.*
Love of letters and letter writing; affection
for the art of epistolography; a sickness
characterized by excessive letter writing.

Contents

Illustrations

Acknowledgments

I could never have written this book without research and writing grants. I thank the following institutions, all of whom supported my work: the Canada Council for the Arts, Le Conseil des arts et lettres du Québec, the Banff Centre for the Arts, the YIVO Institute for Jewish Research, the Money for Women/Barbara Deming Memorial Fund, Yad Vashem's International Institute for Holocaust Research, and the Holocaust Educational Foundation.

I gratefully acknowledge the aid of institutions that hold or have held Šimaitė's papers: Vilnius University Library, Kent State University Archives, the Hoover Institution Archives, Mažvydas Lithuanian National Library, YIVO Archives, and Yad Vashem Archives.

I also thank Kęstutis Šimas, Laima Griciūtė, Vladas Žukas, Eglė Makariūnienė, Nijolė Šulgienė, Alma Masevičienė, Mark Clamen, Heather Lundine, Bridget Barry, Rimantas Stankevičius, Laimonas Briedis, Elena Razlogova, Dan Porat, Shlomo and Merav Tal, Brad Nelson, and Laura Levitt for their kindness and help.

Finally, to Sean Gurd and our son Sebastian: may this book be a love letter to you both.

A Note on Place Names

MOST cities and villages in Lithuania have at least two names: a Lithuanian one, a Yiddish one, and often a Russian or Polish one. I use the name Vilnius to designate the city that is now the capital of Lithuania, though I refer to the Vilna Ghetto and occasionally to Vilna, if the reference is to Jewish culture and community in that city. I use its Polish name, Wilno, once, where the context is the city's Polish history. For the most part, I have reproduced Lithuanian place names as Šimaitė used them in her writing: in Lithuanian. The only other exceptions are Vilnius old town street names (where possible, I offer the Lithuanian followed by the Yiddish equivalent), Kaunas and Kovno (I use the latter when referring to that city's ghetto) and the mass murder site of Paneriai (Lithuanian) or Ponar (Yiddish), in which case I use both names.

1. Ona Šimaitė. Vilnius University Library Rare Books and Manuscripts Department.

Epistolophilia

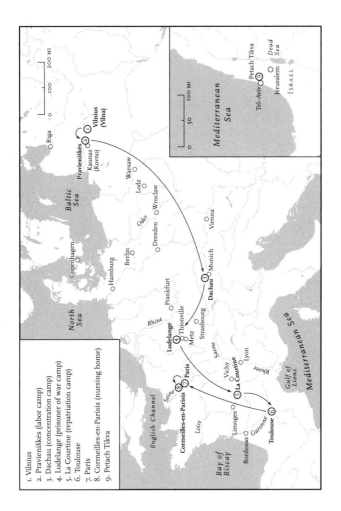

1. Šimaitė's movements from 1939 to 1970. The map shows her journey from Vilnius to Dachau, Ludelange, La Courtine, Toulouse, and Paris. The insert shows Petach Tikva, Israel.

1. Vilnius
2. Pravieniškes (labor camp)
3. Dachau (concentration camp)
4. Ludelange (prisoner of war camp)
5. La Courtine (repatriation camp)
6. Toulouse
7. Paris
8. Cormeilles-en-Parisis (nursing home)
9. Petach Tikva

PART 1

CHAPTER 1

The Woman in the Park

THE year is 2009. I am sitting at my desk at home in Montreal, daydreaming. I let my mind wander. It takes me over the Atlantic and back to the early 1950s. I often travel across time and through imagined spaces like this as I write. It's the only way I can see her, my librarian friend.

Across the street two elderly men sit on a bench together. One is bearded and wears a hat. The other, clean-shaven and bare-headed, wears thick glasses. Deep in a heated discussion, they hardly notice the summer rain. The tree behind the bench shelters them almost completely, and only the odd raindrop lands with a pop on the bearded one's brim. He speaks first, talking for a long time, as if giving a speech, his voice gradually rising to a shout. The companion listens silently, and other than minute twitches, offers no reaction. Only once his friend has finished and sits with pinched lips does he utter a word. From my vantage point I make out little of what they say. The evening breeze carries their voices away, but when then the wind changes direction, fragments of their discussion reach my ears.

". . . here in Paris there's an old Gentile lady, a . . . knows that in the Vilna Ghetto she saved the lives of Jews . . . books . . . sent . . . camp in France. Since . . . Jewish refugees . . . old revolutionist, an atheist; that is to say, she doesn't believe in God."

The bare-headed one continues. He is calmer than his friend, keeping his voice steady and searching the other's face.

"Imagine . . . the old lady . . . sitting here listening to us! . . . don't say anything . . . only listen."

My heart jumps. He could only be referring to her. There's no one else. The wind blows one last sentence to me in its entirety:

"She is not Jewish, but she hid our sacred books."

I recognize the bare-headed one as a Yiddish writer, known for his bad temper and jealousy. But he's brilliant and, judging from the scene playing out before me, softer than his reputation suggests. Despite having once been considered for the Nobel Prize, he died years ago in the relative obscurity that his language imposed on him.

I want to stay longer to hear how the quarrel between the writer and his friend will conclude, but I have an appointment to keep. Every day she comes home by metro and crosses the park to her apartment on the rue de Courcelles. I've been following her for weeks.

Parc Monceau is an eighteenth-century-style garden built by a duke, who was later executed in the French Revolution. Streams run through it, and Corinthian columns still stand in a pond filled with ducks and other birds attracted to this patch of green in the heart of Paris. Willow branches hang over the water. I watch as the belly of a shiny orange fish slips through their reflections.

On weekends Monceau is full of children. Parents sit on benches and talk. They pack picnic lunches and ride with their kids on carousels. Some read quietly in the shade. Tonight the park is almost empty. The rain has now stopped and the benches are wet. A few couples walk hand in hand along paths. One woman feeds the birds and fish morsels of bread. My librarian walks slowly, stopping to admire the park's statues. "Today that beautiful park seems calm, but in 1871 members of the Paris Commune were shot there *en masse*," she wrote in one of her diaries. "To me, this park is both a place of restful beauty and of sanctity" (August 29, 1958, Diary 21).

On hot days she rinses her face and hands at the green fountain by the grass. I keep my distance, observing her as I would an animal. In one arm she carries a loaf of bread, and in the other, her ubiquitous handbag. Today I learned that Claude Monet painted this park five times. Every garden, every street in this city has been marked not only by revolution but by art. The librarian loves to walk the streets that writers walked and to sit in the places that painters studied. In Paris, she often writes in her letters, even a person of the most modest means has access to great beauty.

The lacy iron gate on the far side of the park is only a short walk from her building. Exiting, we pass a curious red façade of dueling dragons and lattice before we descend the gentle slope to Number 38. The building is dated 1927. Carvings of plump peonies adorn its entrance. I hang back and watch her disappear inside as the gate clangs shut. This is as far as I go. Inside, her feet shuffle up stairs, breath heavy as she takes a rest on the second-floor landing. One of those tiny windows at the very top is hers. Eighth floor. Her first impressions of the room were not positive. After spending her first nights there in September 1957, she wrote:

This is the worst room I've ever had. I'm living like a poor clochard in a neighborhood of aristocrats. Up until the sixth floor everything is shiny and clean, with carpets laid out, and there are flowers and a fountain in the courtyard. But once you get to the seventh and eighth floors, it's a total dump. Even if I'd never heard or read anything about class differences — riches and poverty — I would have come up with it myself just by living here. (September 3, 1957, Diary 17)

Plaster crumbles from the ceiling and walls, and she must carry her water down the long narrow hallways to do her laundry, washing, and cooking. She curses the landlady for her greed and lack of compassion, but the move to the new room nonetheless brings one positive development. For a year after her return from Israel, the librarian worked as a servant in return for room and board.

2. Šimaitė's apartment building in Paris. Photo by the author.

(On August 22, 1958, she wrote in her diary, "The French saying resonates deeply: if you give birth to a daughter and you know she will become a servant, it's better to drown her right away." [Diary 21]) She has spent every Thursday of the past year laundering the clothes of her employers. But not anymore. For better or for worse, she will now live alone. Though she never complains of money or food shortages in the letters to her family in Lithuania, the diaries attest to the poverty of her life in Paris:

APRIL 17, 1958
Today I washed two weeks' worth of clothes. The carrying in and out of that water is so difficult, especially when I'm washing black or colorful things. I washed my hair too, which is also no small challenge. I made a soup for lunch and dinner — potatoes, barley, lamb's tongue, onions, parsley. It was delicious. And I drank some tea with chocolate sent from Vilnius. I found it very moving.

I unraveled a sweater, and that alone took four hours. It's good for the rich, they never have to recycle objects. But the poor waste so much time on basic necessities. This is why they have so little energy and time to do good for others and for cultural activities.

As I write, I am soaking my aching legs. And after this, I have to wash the floor and go to the bath house. The bath house is far, and I can't get there and back in less than two and a half hours. (Diary 19)

Every night I wait outside the gates to see which room is hers. I wait for a light, for the window to open, or for her silhouette to appear, but once she passes through the gates, I lose track of her entirely.

Slipping in and out. This is what she does. An old lady with a limp and accent, she is invisible to most. Her face is not obviously that of a warrior or revolutionary, and perhaps this is why she succeeded in a situation that demanded secrecy, courage, and disguise. We know that from 1941 to 1944 she slipped into the Jewish Ghetto of German-occupied Vilnius to bring its prisoners food, clothes, medicine, money, and forged documents. She carried letters and messages. In one case, she brought a vial of strychnine for a friend to use if suicide became his only escape. She came out of the ghetto with letters to deliver and manuscripts to hide. In one case she stole away with a Jewish girl, and on others carried out sedated children in sacks. Occasionally she spent the night in the ghetto, sharing a bed with her opera-singing friend on evenings when she attended the ghetto's concerts, plays, and art exhibits. She supported its most desperate by listening to their fears and responding to their letters — in most cases, the last ones they ever wrote. We do not know how many lives she saved (though a 1963 article published in an Argentinean-Lithuanian newspaper writes that her actions saved "around one hundred Jewish children from certain starvation in the ghetto." She copied the article into her diary).[1] To keep a tally would have been out of character for the librarian, and a systematic forgetting of the names and addresses of those she helped was her way of protecting herself and others. What we have instead are individual stories, anecdotes, and reminiscences of survivors.

In 1944 the Gestapo detected the librarian's activities. They arrested her and tortured her for twelve days, then deported her to the prison camp at Dachau. She survived and moved to Paris after the war, where she worked sporadically as a librarian, a vocation she called "the beloved profession" (Šimaitė, "Lost and Found in Vilna" 313). In 1966 Yad Vashem, Israel's official memorial to Jewish Holocaust victims, honored the librarian as Righteous Among the Nations. She died in 1970. Her name was Ona Šimaitė.

Šimaitė's writings speak to me in a familiar voice. Her language has the cadence and vocabulary of my grandmother's Lithuanian. But, unlike *Močiutė*, who now lives in a past inside her head, Šimaitė seems curiously contemporary. Wry, kind, funny, and sometimes angry, her letters are riveting and inspire an immediate feeling of kinship. When I read them I feel as though she is speaking to me directly, that these letters have been saved specifically for me, and that I have a responsibility to her, this friend from another era. But it isn't only about what I can do for her. Through her letters and diaries, Šimaitė has answered questions about the Holocaust in Lithuania that have dogged me since my teenaged years. How was it that so many people were killed? Why was our community so silent about the German occupation? Or the Jewish community in Lithuania? Šimaitė was the first person to speak to me frankly on these subjects in the language of my childhood. And through her letters, she offered a window to a place and time that had remained frustratingly shrouded.

For almost a decade I have followed Šimaitė's paper trail to Lithuania and Israel and across the United States, where her writings are archived. When I began this journey, this relationship with a ghost, I was still a student. After the first discovery of Šimaitė's manuscripts in Vilnius, I started to think about what it meant to write a woman's life, the life of this woman who, except to those who knew her and what she had done during a period of three years in Lithuania, had gone through life largely unseen. Šimaitė's story has led me to consider questions of self-sacrifice, creativity, and the feminine; of what is expected of a woman and how these expectations may change her relationship to herself; how women write their lives publicly, privately, and why; and of choices we make every day between life and death.

CHAPTER 2

Vilnius

IN the spring of 2000 I rented a tiny studio apartment in Vilnius, just off the city's main boulevard. The apartment was all white, with hardwood floors and a loft so close to the ceiling I couldn't sit up in bed without hitting my head. The builders in the court-yard started work at the crack of dawn each morning, rousing me from sleep, so Vilnius days started earlier than usual. Before 8:30 I would head off to work in the manuscript department of the national library of Lithuania. It was there that I found the first collection of manuscripts. One cool May morning, I was looking up names in the card catalog randomly and unsuccessfully, until I tried "Šimaitė." It was a name I knew only in passing, having come across it in my dissertation research on writings about the Vilna Ghetto. Sure enough, hundreds of cards nestled behind this name. The find marked the beginning of a journey that would take me around the world to collect the librarian's papers, scattered over three countries and as many continents.

Most of Šimaitė's writings consist of letters in either Lithuanian or Russian, though a small number are in Polish, French, and German, plus twenty-nine postwar diaries, and a dozen or so articles. The Lithuanian letters I collected in Vilnius in 2000 date mostly from the 1950s and '60s, and tell primarily of an exchange of books with friends in Soviet Lithuania. They are almost silent on the subject that has made the librarian famous among Holocaust survivors and historians, telling little about what she did during the Nazi occupation of Vilnius, or her torture and imprisonment. The full collection starts in 1932 and ends in 1970, when Šimaitė died in a home for the elderly on the outskirts of Paris. The early years, from 1932–1945 are sparse — much was lost, destroyed, or confiscated — but the 1945 and 1946 files are thick, and almost everything in them is in Russian, Šimaitė's third or fourth language, depending on how you count. To read them I needed to resurrect linguistic skills that had gone unused for ten years, and I chose a lengthy typescript to work through first, reasoning this would be an easier reintroduction to Cyrillic than the handwritten letters of the rest of the file. Slowly I begin reacquainting myself with the sounds and symbols of Russian: the *yoos* (ю), *yahs* (я), the guttural *khs* (x), and the letter *shtch* (щ) that sounds like a quick sneeze.

At first I could only decipher one paragraph of the Russian typescript per day. The process was exhausting. I stared at a word on the page, knowing that somewhere deep in the recesses of my memory its meaning must still be stored but, unable to retrieve it, I found myself turning to dictionaries for the simplest and most elementary of phrases. But over time my reading sped up, the letter began to reveal itself, and the process started to offer rewards. By the end of six months I'd managed to work my way through the eighty-eight-page document. It opened with the arrival of the Nazis in Vilnius on June 23, 1941:

Four o'clock in the morning. The sounds of shells exploding could be heard in the distance. Shooting could be heard somewhere very close by. Shootings had been heard for some time already, every day at four or five o'clock in the morning. They went from house to house, snatching young Jewish men and women whom they suspected of Bolshevism, and they executed them early in the morning.

Within a few days of the Nazis' arrival, orders directed at Jews began to appear one after another, as if from a horn of plenty. Bit by bit, they

Vilnius

apparently sought to break the moral and physical strength of the Jewish resistance. (Šimaitė in Šukys "And I burned" 19)

Šimaitė describes hundreds of people climbing over barriers to board the last train leaving for Soviet territory. She offers her account of the city's ghettoization, together with a story of smuggling wood-burning stoves and other necessities into the ghetto with the passive help of ghetto police's blind eye. She tells of the underground press, of anti-Semitic posters that equated Bolsheviks with Jews, and of hateful caricatures displayed in bookstore windows enumerating supposed Jewish offences against Lithuanians. Finally, she recounts managing to hide people in her Vilnius apartment and at the university library.

From the typescript I moved on to Šimaitė's Russian manuscripts. There were letters to friends and family of those who had not survived the ghetto. They described the suffering and resolve of the ghetto prisoners, and passed on messages of farewell. The letters contained images from Šimaitė's new life in France, and told of her difficulty finding a job and a place to live. In them she worried for her family in Lithuania, and responded to rumors that the Gestapo had killed her.

By the end of her life, Šimaitė wrote almost exclusively in Lithuanian, her native tongue. It is a language that few non-linguists know a lot about. It is often assumed that Lithuanian, a language of some 3.5 million speakers, has a great deal in common with and must be closely related to Russian, but this is not the case. The two languages are about as close as Spanish and English, or Norwegian and French. They fall under the same broad linguistic umbrella — Indo-European — but belong to distinct subcategories: Russian is Slavic, and Lithuanian is Baltic. Lithuanian, like English, is written in Latin letters, but contains a few diacritics, like the tiny *v* above the *S* in Šimaitė's name. (Lithuanians call this a *paukštelis*, 'a little bird.') The letter *š* in Šimaitė's name is pronounced *sh*, as in 'should' or 'shoe.' The letter *ė* represents a sound more difficult for most English speakers to reproduce. It's a long, flat sound, sort of like the *a* sound in ale or the Canadian *eh?*, but without the lilting upturn at the end. The *ai* of her name is said in exactly the same way that Leonard Cohen (whose grandfather, incidentally, was a rabbi in Lithuania) sings "ay, ay-yay-yay" (take this waltz, take this waltz . . .). So: Šimaitė is said *Shim-ay-teh*.

I live in a place where French is the daily language, and even though it interpenetrates with English here in Montreal, linguistic lines are still drawn with surprising severity. When I was pregnant with my son, I mentioned to an anglophone friend that I wanted to give him a name that would travel easily across languages. She looked at me and asked, in all seriousness, why? But it's not only English speakers who see little point in accommodating or taking stock of the other. When I was eighteen I spent a few months in France intensively learning the language, and was one day corrected by a teacher on how to pronounce my own surname. *En français S se prononce ssss*, (In French, S is pronounced *ssss,*) she said. I replied, *Mais Madame, mon nom n'est pas français* (But Madam, my surname isn't French). She ignored me.

Like Šimaitė's, my surname is Lithuanian. Judging from the requests for linguistic help that come across my desk, some Holocaust historians view the language as a nuisance. Their emails betray an annoyance at the fact that documents in or from Lithuania should be written in Lithuanian, that Lithuanian archives should be catalogued in Lithuanian, and that Lithuanian archivists should speak Lithuanian. In *Vilna on the Seine*, Judith Friedlander describes the status of two ancient languages held to be the two closest living relatives to Sanskrit thus: "Missing from this impressive list of languages [spoken by Litvak intellectuals] are Latvian and Lithuanian, for in this world of polyglots, where the Jewish middle classes spoke five and six tongues, nobody bothered to learn the 'dialects' of the peasants" (165).

The exoticism with which the language and region is viewed

often verges on the absurd. In a passage describing his mother's passport in *Heshel's Kingdom*, Dan Jacobson, whose Lithuanian-Jewish family left for South Africa before World War II, almost certainly saving their lives, writes of a stamp he finds among the passport's pages: "Of yet another visa I can make no sense at all; it seems to have been issued by a country called Skyrius, which I cannot believe ever existed. Not even there. Not even then. Perhaps it was nothing more than [an] exit visa from Lithuania" (50). The Lithuanian word "skyrius," of course, simply means "department," as in Department of Foreign Affairs, or Visa Department. I read this passage long ago, more than ten years ago now, but it has stayed with me as an illustration of the laughable, quaint, and isn't-it-cute status that a small language like Lithuanian continues to have. Not even there! Not even in this land of funny people with made-up languages, hard-to-pronounce names, and fantastical places! I bristle when asked if "we really need to include all those squiggles and dots in the place names," because the person inquiring would never remove an accent from a French or German equivalent. When met with a comment on the weirdness of my father's or aunt's names, I fight to keep an even tone of voice when offering a reminder that in Lithuania these names are perfectly normal, and that there (and sometimes even in Montreal) my husband's name, Sean, seems unpronounceable. And all of this only makes me wonder if Šimaitė had been born in Germany or France, and if her name had been Anna Strauss or Anne Simard, and if she'd written her diaries and journals in a major Western European language, perhaps someone would have written about her decades ago.

Born in a Lithuanian village called Akmenė in 1894, Šimaitė came from a family more likely to work as domestics than to employ them. After World War II, she joined the invisible Paris population that cleaned, ironed, laundered, and kept the city's more noticeable inhabitants presentable. By the 1950s and '60s, she had acquired an impressive list of languages — Lithuanian, Latvian, Polish, Russian,

German, French, and a bit of Hebrew — and was at ease living and writing in and out of all of them. She loved France, and Paris in particular, because the government there did not force her to choose a citizenship. In Paris she was happy to live as a stateless person.

As things stand, Šimaitė is marginal to everything: to her adopted home of France, to Russian culture, to Yiddish culture, to Israel, and because of her class, gender, and native language, to historical and literary interest.

When faced with a figure like Šimaitė, who fits no categories — not even that of a writer! — what do we do? How do we tell her story?

Making her matter to anyone other than me might be a tall order.

CHAPTER 3

Correspondence

AFTER World War II, Šimaitė corresponded with poets, novelists, friends, admirers, and fellow librarians, writing an average of sixty letters each month. A survey of her correspondents reveals a cast of characters wildly varied in age and experience. They include the musicology student Vytautas Landsbergis (Lithuania's first post-Soviet president); Tayda Devėnaitė, the head of Lithuania's Valstybinė grožinės literatūros leidykla (State Literary Publishing House); relatives in Lithuania; the former diplomat Juozas Urbšys; the Litvak writer Icchokas Meras; and survivors in Israel, Poland, North America, South America, and France, including Marc Dworzhetsky, who was gathering testimony about the Vilna Ghetto in the late 1940s and '50s.

One of Šimaitė's longest correspondences was with Vytautas Kauneckas, a translator living in Vilnius. Theirs was a tumultuous relationship revolving around the sending of a multivolume *Larousse* dictionary from France to Soviet Lithuania, an exchange that involved a complicated accounting system measured in books sent, duty paid, and rubles delivered to Šimaitė's relatives in Lithuania. Several times Šimaitė tried to break off the correspondence because of accounting disputes and general fatigue from the pressure she felt from the growing pile of unanswered letters on her desk. Her translator friend, she complained, suffered from

3. Šimaitė's letters. Vilnius University Library Rare Books and Manuscripts Department.

a dictionary-collecting syndrome, never getting enough of them and requiring more and more, while she herself had become the enabler of his addiction: "You may be angry and offended, or not, but I maintain my earlier opinion — you suffer from a dictionary mania. And I blame myself for my own madness of sending you those dictionaries and enabling your illness" (February 24, 1964, Kauneckas's Papers).

The Kauneckas correspondence is occasionally quite funny, but we learn from her correspondence with Juozas Urbšys, with whom she also exchanged books, that Kauneckas was a broken man. His sentence to a Siberian labor camp because of his writing remained a trauma that lay at the heart of his physical and, according to Šimaitė, psychological troubles later in life. Besides books, a major theme in the Kauneckas correspondence is schizophrenia. His daughter, Sigita, suffered from the disease and from 1968 to

4. Vytautas Kauneckas. The Translator sent this photograph to Šimaitė. On the back he inscribed: "Kulautuva. June 30, 1959. I am in my room. Everything you see on the table, my dear Ona, was sent by you." Vilnius University Library, Rare Books and Manuscripts Department.

1970 was continually in and out of mental institutions shuttling back and forth between her estranged parents' homes. Šimaitė's niece too suffered from schizophrenia and she often sent the Translator, as she called him in her family correspondence, on missions to evaluate the young woman's state. In return, Šimaitė sent French articles and books outlining the latest findings on schizophrenia.

After the war Šimaitė's main concern was to secure locations for texts about the destruction of the Litvaks and their culture. She worked tirelessly sending copies of Icchokas Meras's novels to the Centre de documentation juive contemporaine (Contemporary Jewish Documentation Center) in Paris, to the Ghetto Fighters' House, and the Jewish National and University Libraries in Israel. She was equally concerned that American and Israeli publications and other books she valued find their way into libraries in Soviet Lithuania. When Soviet customs seized some of these as contraband, the librarian learned firsthand about the government's anti-Semitic policies and the ins and outs of Soviet censorship.

Šimaitė's Lithuanian-language correspondence and diaries are remarkable in that she rarely mentions the events in Nazi-occupied Vilnius that stamped her life so decisively, or the actions with which she saved the lives of others. There are only masked and obscure references: she refers to "my errands," to "those people," to nothing concrete, and to no one by name.

But an instinct to archive was bred into her, and in a letter to a friend she stressed how dear "every scrap of printed paper" was to a librarian (December 17, 1957, Šimaitė's Papers, Mažvydas). At the end of her life she was fastidious about ascertaining that her letters and articles be safeguarded in archives and began to catalog and organize her papers, whose content impressed even her: "What letters!! I have many treasures like this in my archives. Yesterday I devoted six hours to them. But I don't feel hunger when I work with my archives" (July 26, 1969, Diary 28). Yet, even while recognizing the importance of her experiences, after the war she avoided writing of the ghetto or camps. The notes and letters that have survived contain few clues about the events that have secured Šimaitė a place in historical recollection.

Throughout Šimaitė's postwar correspondence there are numerous requests for her to write her memoirs. Of particular note are the requests of Marijona Čilvinaitė, with whom she had a most interesting epistolary relationship, and whom she sent in search of hidden documents at the Vilnius University Library. After reestablishing contact with Šimaitė in the late 1950s, Čilvinaitė began to collect Šimaitė's letters from family and friends, depositing them in the manuscript department at the Mažvydas National Library of Lithuania (Čilvinaitė's letter to Devėnaitė, December 22, 1960, Čilvinaitė's Papers). Again and again, Čilvinaitė asked her friend to write about her experiences in the Vilna Ghetto and of her internment in Dachau, impressing on her that the experiences and friendships they'd had together as young women now made up the fabric of history: "My dear Onutė, running along the path of life, you don't stop and think that you're dashing through the pages of history" (November 9, 1968, Čilvinaitė's Papers). Similarly, she wrote to Šimaitė on New Year's Eve, 1958:

You write that I experienced a lot during the war. True, but you can't compare my experiences with the tortures you suffered over the murder of innocent, totally innocent people. If you've [written] anything, I'd like you to send me something about your arrest, interrogation, torture in the concentration camps, and so on. Not for idle curiosity's sake, but for the knowledge of how evil a scourge raged through Europe in the 20th century. (December 31, 1957–January 1, 1958, Čilvinaitė's Papers)

Later in that same letter Čilvinaitė asked about the fate of a Jewish girl who used to come to her house, and who was beaten one day when caught smuggling flour and applesauce into the ghetto for her mother. Šimaitė's response to Čilvinaitė's letter is extraordinary in that she talks about her own internment in Dachau very briefly, but in some detail. It is one of a handful of mentions of her concentration camp experience in her letters:

My Dear Marytė, Folktale,[1] the suffering endured was immeasurable. Everyone had his or her share in those murderous times. It's always easier for me to suffer personally than to see others suffer, whom I can't help. The girl you mentioned in your letter, like an uncountable number of other people, died.

Perhaps one day I will write about my arrest, interrogation, and experiences in the concentration camp. As long as I'm alive, I'll never forget how, after 10 or 11 hours of hard work, they laid the Roma children on trestles and whipped them. It's too horrible to remember. Sometimes I'd like to believe that it wasn't real, just a horrible dream. Together with me they transported Roma men to the camp, young men, strong as oak trees. But after three months they were invalids, and walked with sticks. As soon as they could no longer walk home, a black truck drove up and they disappeared without a trace. Or again, that horrible "aufstehen," when the guards would beat on the doors with clubs at 3:30 in the morning. . . .[2]

I don't know if I'll have the strength to write my memoirs. . . . When I get a place in the home for the elderly I'll start re-writing that manuscript [that was lost in Vilnius], so that some sort of image shall remain. I'd like that memoir-work to be preserved in the archive. (February 5, 1958, Čilvinaitė's Papers)

By 1960, despite her good intentions and promises, Šimaitė had not yet managed to produce even a small piece of her memoir. Perhaps it was simply too painful, or perhaps (and there seems to be some evidence to support this when Šimaitė emphasizes that survivors will write the history of the ghettos far better than she), to claim that her actions were in any way special went against the grain. Time and energy eventually ran out, and Šimaitė left us without completing a memoir. But this is not to say that she left us without an inheritance.

Šimaitė left an impressive archive of her life's writing: thousands of letters, scores of postwar diaries and notebooks, various articles and countless press clippings. Faced with this massive record, I am confronted by the question of how to read this proliferation of papers. What clues are there in this mountain of documents as to how to proceed with an interpretation of this intriguing yet frustrating collection of personal writings?

Her correspondence tells a remarkable story, one that challenges a number of common assumptions in scholarly thinking about memory, the importance of writing as a life-structuring practice, the significance of silence in a body of work, and the literariness of private and female texts.

5. Marijona Čilvinaitė. F64-226. Mažvydas National Library of Lithuania Rare
Books and Manuscripts Department.

CHAPTER 4

Ona Šimaitė's Letters to Marijona Čilvinaitė, 1957–1958

OCTOBER 2, 1957

Dearest Marytė! How much you and your loved ones have suffered! It was difficult to read your remembrances of those terrible war years without tears. What surprises me most about that hell is people's solidarity in helping others. But you write nothing about what happened to your father. I would very much like for him to be alive, healthy, because the two of us were of one mind and one heart when it came to, as they say, the Jewish question. . . . If he's alive, bow down low to him for me.[1] If he's dead — may the sweet earth of Lithuania lie lightly on him!

There's so much I would like to write to you about, and I don't even know where to start. Of course, I won't be able to tell you everything in one letter, so the rest will remain for others. I think this is neither the first nor the last letter.

First of all, it makes me very happy that you are working in the beloved profession, and that you have no material worries. May you always be well, Marytė.

The sprig of rue and the wildflower enclosed in the letter brought me great pleasure. . . .

It's difficult for me to write to you, because so many memories arise as I write. . . . To this day I have no idea what happened after my arrest. Normally the Nazis confiscated everything and emptied out one's room. I'm most concerned for some books and manuscripts — some mine and others not mine — that were left at home. Did any of these things get left behind in my room? It happened that just before my arrest I had brought home the manuscript of my book of poetry . . . I would like to have it so much. . . .

I'm sorry for the loss of a great many things. If you know anything about these things, sit down to write to me.

I didn't write any memoirs about the ghetto while I was still in Vilnius, but I did make some notes. I actually had some material that I had collected in the ghetto, and it (in my opinion) was quite valuable, as well as 200 letters that had been written to me from the ghetto. Some other people knew where I had put them. But they told me that the war destroyed everything. Nevertheless, I have some doubts. Perhaps they were destroyed, or perhaps someone took them. Marytė, I trust you 100%. If you could dedicate some time and at least check for what I hid in the Lithuanian philology seminar room at the university. It may all be for nothing. It would be an incredible shame if everything had disappeared. If you really can help, then help, and in the next letter I'll tell you where to look. But I repeat — there's little hope that anything survived.

While living in Paris I started to write about the Vilna Ghetto. The problem is that I know a great deal, but I'm unable to write it all down. And now there's no great need for me to do so, since the surviving Jews will tell it, and they have already written about it to such an extent that one can only marvel.

Of what I've written, the section "My Correspondence with the People of the Vilna Ghetto" turned out the best. It has been translated into Yiddish and Hebrew and published.

I'd like to clean up what I've written, and Mrs. Jaffa, the wife of a famous poet in Haifa, has promised to type it for me. She will transcribe it, send it to 4 Israeli organizations, as well as to some international Jewish organizations. I'll ask her to make one more copy for the Soviet Lithuanian University's Library.

I want to clean up the written material by the New Year — I don't know whether or not I'll succeed. But I won't write any more than I've already written.

Different articles of mine about the Vilna Ghetto have been published in the Jewish press in America, Argentina, Israel and South Africa, as well as in Paris. But I don't have the originals anymore. I write them and then give them away like letters.

In Israel I was given a life-long pension and accommodation. But I was sick from the heat. I returned to Paris after 3 years.

At times life was indescribably difficult for me here. Because the world's artistic treasures are so accessible here, I help myself to them by the handful.

Now my life has become somewhat easier. A certain Jewish organization has given me a stipend until the New Year. So now I work at the library only 3 days, and after taking care of my health and the library work, I want to use the remaining time to clean up my notes, to write letters and to prepare my sewing lessons. I'd like to get as much done as possible; I fear sickness more than anything. Even now, the flu has taken strong hold of me. This is a letter written in haste. Oh, Marytė, what interesting and varying libraries I've worked in. I work in one for a few months, then later on I'm recommended to another. I organized an incredible amount of material on art in those libraries; the Englishman Smith (his charcoal drawings), the German impressionists, and all the material about Goya from his lifetime have especially stayed in my memory. One library was organized according the construction of a steamer. Generally, I used to visit all the big libraries in every city. But now I don't have the strength to do that anymore, except with the greatest difficulty. My legs work very badly now.

Well, take care. I plan to write again. And you write to me.

I kiss you.

Ona

DECEMBER 17, 1957

Dear Marytė! I promised to write you a letter promptly. But rivers of time have flowed by and not a word. Please forgive my long silence. On the occasion of the upcoming New Year, I want to wish you good health, and many good and beautiful rays of life. In France it's tradition to give little calendars + a little something for New Year's. But I can only send you, dearest, a small little calendar. Every printed item is dear to every librarian. Therefore, accept this small calendar as sincerely as I send it to you. . . .

I'm following with great interest the impressive cultural life taking place in Lithuania. Beautiful periodicals fill my life's days. I bow down to the people who are accomplishing such great cultural work.

[A friend in Lithuania] sent me a reference book called "Kaunas." I learned a lot from it and saw things I've never seen before, which once again brought me great joy. I'm especially happy that the Kaunas University Library has such a rich manuscript collection.

In February I'm entering a home for the elderly, where I will receive my meals and will have my own little room. Then I'll clean up those notes that I've written and send them to the library's manuscript department. But they're written in Russian. I think that the most successful one is "My Correspondence with the People of the Vilna Ghetto." Though it would have been more accurate to call it "Letters from People of the Vilna Ghetto." I would very much like for this to make it to the manuscript department. The cannibalistic past must not be forgotten. I can't undertake this work until I move into the home. I barely have enough strength to earn my daily bread and to take care of my personal health.

The text that I was telling you about above is about 41 pages long and was published in Yiddish, as well as "Liuba Levitska — Nightingale of the Ghetto," which appeared in a women's worker magazine in Hebrew. If you write me that it's worth keeping these in the manuscript department, I'll send you some other things I've written as well, once I've finished cleaning it up. But for now, it will have to wait.

There's little hope that anything is left of what I had hidden in the Lithuanian philology seminar room's library. Other people knew about it as well, and they probably removed it and perhaps, out of fear or for other reasons, destroyed it. There's little hope, but these things are very important to me. No one knows the Lithuanian philology seminar room better than you. Please take a day off and go to Vilnius. It's possible that something's still there. When you exit the seminar, there's a small cellar under the stairs. There used to be all kinds of junk there. I hid the letters written to me, some of my notes — observations, as well as some newspaper clippings under that junk. If by some miracle something were left — don't throw anything away without me, and I'll explain to you why this or that newspaper clipping is included. Go upstairs to the attic — and on the right, where the roof slopes down [a tiny diagram is drawn here], there's a metal box buried, which contains G. Šuras's notes about the Vilna Ghetto. I was told that this attic is no longer there. But for some reason I don't believe it. I very much want for these things to be found, even though so many years have gone by. Try to look for them. If you didn't find anything, don't regret your efforts. There's little hope, but there's still some sort of tiny crystal of hope — maybe something's there? I think you understand me well.

[Written up the margin] Did you succeed in fixing things with Chomskis?

Take care, help me. I kiss you.

Sincerely Ona

FEBRUARY 5, 1958

Dear Folktale-Marytė! I received your sweet, sincere letter written on May 7th a long time ago.

It moved me very much, because with it my final hope died. I thank you, the library's director, and dear Berželionis for your efforts. It's very painful for me. I thought that nothing would be left, because I was not the only one who knew where the manuscript was hidden. Maybe it was emptied out of there as soon as I was arrested. After the war one person told me that the roof wasn't even there anymore. Apparently, the seminar roof hasn't suffered at all. And to bring all that out of the ghetto was so risky. I know that the other hiding places were destroyed by bombs. Not only manuscripts perished, but people as well. It makes me happy that the seminar room gave shelter to two people. Professor Mowszowicz stayed there for two days and two nights, and Sala Vaksman, a hidden student, lived there for 7½ months. Both survived. Dear Berželionis had to scheme and convince the other library workers that I, a library employee, was under doctor's orders to sweep the seminar room and its staircase for health reasons. In doing this, even he, Berželionis, contributed to the saving of one life. Let this be my best greeting to him.

Oh, Marytė, what terrible times those were. Sometimes it seems impossible that this could have happened in my life, that it's just a chilling dream. . . .

Take care, Dear Marytė. Love me with all my vices.

Kisses.

Sincerely yours,

Ona

Travailler pour ce monde comme
si vous deviez toujours y vivre,
et pour l'autre comme si vous
deviez mourir demain.
           Proverbe arabe.

6/iv Šeštadienis Algyvento 6 ~~tad~~. šįt mėn dienos.
Kasdie viški nysičiai ir nidarkiai del
duonos kasnio — toukdo gyventi pagal
išminčių aralų falasle.
        Daktarai uždraudė sunkų fizinį darbą,
o reikia kas savaitę ir skalbti ir laidyti!
Biblioteko archyve darbas neidomus, daugiau
technuškos. Po sunkaus darbo — tie prakeikimai
ir vyksmai svejos, kad paėmiau duonos
šmolelį su sviestu vakarinei. Juk aš
uždirbu valgį kruvinu darbu — skalbymas
laidymas. Taip ji mane įžeidė, kad geriau
badauti, arba pirkti iš savo skatikus.
Bet už skatikų aš taip nedaug feudirbu
bibliotekoje. Ir dirbu dabar bibliotekoje
1 d. manierus, kad galėčiau šitą pamokti
sintis pamokromis. Na, ir skolas reikia
kas mėnesi mokėti iš vaišbus.
        Buvau išbaigusi, per kuriū paminėjau

CHAPTER 5

Caregiving and Letters

IN addition to thousands of letters, Šimaitė left twenty-nine diaries covering the period from 1953 to 1970: two record the year of 1953 in Paris; ten document 1953–1956 in Israel; and seventeen cover 1956–1970 in Paris. They record the minutiae of Šimaitė's life: food and money shortages, laundry, and the drudgery of work are constant themes. But above all, the diaries record Šimaitė's compulsive letter-writing. A good example can be found in Diary 17 from the year 1957. The very first entry starts with a quotation that Šimaitė identifies as an Arabic proverb: "Work for this world as if you had to live here forever, and for the next as if you had to die tomorrow":

APRIL 6, SATURDAY

Survived six days of this month. Daily problems and the work I do to earn a bite of bread prevent me from living according to the wise Arabic proverb.

The doctors have forbidden me any physical exertion, yet the laundry and ironing must be done every week. Work in the library archives has become impossible, too technical. And after a hard day of work there is the cook swearing and screaming at me for taking a piece of buttered bread for my supper. Don't I earn my meals with this backbreaking work — laundering and ironing? . . .

I wrote letters to both Aldutės [her nieces], and to my two sisters, and today I finally answered that letter, saying I couldn't take part in the discussion in the press, since it's difficult for me even to answer a normal letter in time. But in those 6 days I wrote 14 letters. (September 30, 1957, Diary 17)

Šimaitė kept meticulous count of how many letters she had written and to whom.

The margins of her diaries are filled with numbers that represent how many letters she wrote on any given day. Here, for example, Šimaitė tallies her letters and parcels for the month:

Last Tuesday — September 24 [1957] was a very productive day. I wrote all the letters I had planned to my relatives. Of course, I wasn't able to write to everyone. . . . In all I prepared 67 letters and packages and took them to the post office. Of course, I should have done more, but couldn't. . . .[1] (Diary 17)

This second example, written approximately two months before her death, gives only the month of November as an indication as to when it was written:

I've been sick since October 17. . . . With one exception my heaviest memory will be each and every one of my present and past confrontations with these so-called nurses. They call me names or give me such harsh orders, and yesterday they threw awful accusations at me. They outdo even Hitler's Gestapo — even they didn't order me around like this or keep blaming me. . . . Yesterday I wrote 3 letters dealing with very difficult . . . matters. . . . Last month I received 66 letters and packages, and wrote 67 + one package to my relatives. (Diary 17)

Šimaitė's comparison of the nurses with the Gestapo is striking in its hyperbole, but it illustrates her difficult relationship with caregivers. As she wrote in a 1965 letter, "I am of the opinion that every person must know how to take care of him- or herself. Only in extraordinary circumstances, when it is impossible to help oneself, should one approach others" (Letter to Icchokas Meras, November 20, 1965, Meras's Papers).

But Šimaitė herself was an extreme and eternal caregiver. If people were in pain, she took it upon herself to look after them. In Israel she spent her free days visiting terminally ill patients, bringing them food, reading to them, and teaching the young women to sew dolls. In her diaries she referred to one young woman, for whom she had the most affection, simply as the "ligonė" (the patient):

raistus sergančiai Blaukei, bet vėn kitos
savaitės pabaigoje bus panisti. Manau,
jog 15/V vis tik gaus. Susinervinau, u remiga,
Tokie baisus sapnai mane kankino nakti
del mano giminės senai. Kad galėčiau
pradėti, kad galėčiau nuvažinoti. Dėl
ilgiuosiu jo, nerimauju.

Parašiau laiškus abiem Stasidems, u
abiem ceserims, u tik šiandien atsakiau
į laišką, kad negaliu bendra darbiautis
spaudoje, nes sunku man laiku net į
paprastu laišku atsakyti. Bet per tas
(14) 6 dienas parašiau 14 laiškus. Padėkavojau
šiandien Marius už pinigus.

Trečiadienis mačiau vis iš no pamoku u
buvau mokykloje. Džiaugiu iu ilsės
siela mokykloje.

10/V Trečiadienis. Pasimokiau pamokai, visą antra-
kiau parudai. Net u sirimas, kuris yra
valdišku dokumentu uno menduojamas, mane
labai vargina. Nuo sekmadienio iki šio
dienos 4V vis sirvau. Ir esu taip pavargusi.
Neži nau, ar atpažigsiu iki 7 v. v. kokiu

7. Details from Šimaitė's diaries. The numbers in the margins represent how
many letters she wrote in a given day. Vilnius University Library Rare Books and
Manuscripts Department.

nežmoniškai! Nėra nei kur pasisukti, nei
kur ką padėti. O vienatvė dar didesnė,
negu pas L... Esu nežmoniškai pavargusi,
o pasilsėti nėra kada. Kaip rūgniškai
aiškiai, reikia duoną užsidirbti, sutvar-
kyti visus kasdieniškus savo reikalus —
trūksta laiko ir jėgos...

Bet šį ketvirtadienį nebuvo tokios
baudžiavos, kaip skalbimas. Net savo skal-
binius šią savaitę neskalbiau. Bet buvau
pas Andrė, ilgai kalbėjaus su ja, ten
išprosavojau sijonuką ir priejuostę. Tie
patys seni skudurai, o visai kitaip atrodo
po išprosavojimo.

Ar turėsiu ką valgyti be baudžiavos-
skalbimo? Taip nedaug uždirbu bibliotekoj,
nors ir dirbsiu daugiau dienų. Gysti atgal-
į fizinę ir moralinę vergiją? Kur L daug
moka už mano maitinimą, o mane
skriaudžia ir niekina, ir apvagia.

(7)
+ 3
(10)
Parašiau tik per tas dienas 7 laiškus.
Vienas iš jų 12 pusl. — tai atsiminimai
apie 4 dienas praleistas Italijoje. Daug
pareikalavo laiko, nes rašiau su juod-
raščiu. Daugiau išgyventa, negu galima

susirimo kursus. Kų aš labiausia norėčiau,
kad tie pinigai atneštų man laimę – rasti
laiko mokti susirimo pamokas.

Buvo ir laiškas nuo šeimininkės. Jau įgaliavau
del nusimeldavimo. Stai degulo iš aukštas
į medaus baškulė. Kokie kančia tie vaikiojimai.

Vakar dar parašiau 4 lietiniausius laiškus
(6) +1 ir šiandien 2 – Alei nutei ir Fejai.
(7)   Dar 2 val. iki važiavimo į darbą. Ar
daug sepadaysiu, kada taip salpna ir
truputi karščioju? Kad nebūtų blogiau,
negu yra?

    – "Dyma, kanoro censos mas rusbe?" –
taip rašo Feja viename iš savo atvirukų,
eilėraščis, ir tai šventa teisyga.

    Iki darbo spėjau parašyti Ciloriniatki:

87/x   Antradienis.
            Vėl atgyventa "atkentėta" – 6 dienos.
Atlikau visus kasdylinius ir sarstbaugos darbus,
išskyrus pirties ir galvos plovimo. Labai jau
kankina gripas... Parašyte 13 lietiniausis
laiškus... Kas svarbiausia + tiauriousia
ir sunkiausia – užsimeldavau nuvaděj.
Del šio reikalo sugaišau 4 valandas
vieno ryto. Visas kas 4 val. ant kojis –

8. Šimaitė in Israel. Vilnius University Library Rare Books and Manuscripts Department.

MARCH 18 [1956], SUNDAY

I went to see the ligonė *on Friday morning. There's now a fourth patient in her room, who was howling like an animal from pain. But no one paid her any attention. It went on all night. Finally, one patient's husband couldn't take it anymore, and went to look for help. He found a doctor, etc. That place could drive a healthy person crazy. One journalist, who is also a patient, asked the doctor how long it takes to go insane. The doctor answered: "who knows, maybe you already started going crazy yesterday."*

I'm amazed that my student is still alive and hasn't gone out of her mind.

Another paralyzed patient couldn't get anyone to bring him a bedpan. And not because the nurses are neglectful, but because they're overworked, and there are too few of them. . . .

I pity the people who live there. And I'm so afraid that the same fate will await me, when I can no longer care for myself. (Diary 13)

How do my actions impact others? Who is depending on me? What is my responsibility to those weaker than me? How can I make choices that do not hurt others? These are the questions Šimaitė used as her guide in life. Like so many women, Šimaitė lived according to an ethic of care and a sense of responsibility for the well-being of the world. Her sense of duty toward others extended beyond friends, family, and national boundaries.

But in contrast to this selflessness and generosity, Šimaitė's post-war diaries reveal a downright grumpiness at the burden that others have become in her life. Like any caregiver's, Šimaitė's attitude toward her care work fluctuated as she struggled to find a balance between intellectual ambitions and the responsibility she felt toward others.

In the end, her frustration with caregiving, repetitive work, and a sense of obligation melded with her experience of letter writing. The one thing she wished she could do more of — writing — began to oppress her, and she called herself a martyr to the letter:

NOVEMBER 12 [1955]

Oh, how tormented I was during those three days by various household tasks and the fifteen letters I wrote. Each one of them required between one and two hours' work. And each one deals with a different theme. Sometimes I'm

35

proud that I am able to correspond with a monk. But at the end of the day, I'm a letter martyr. I would like to get rid of my correspondents as quickly as possible and only maintain a small, friendly correspondence with a few people. I get very tired from writing letters, especially the well-written ones which require a lot of heart and nerves, and from the ones I write out of obligation, which I have to write whether or not I want to. (Diary 13)

Šimaitė wrote the final entry in her diary in ballpoint pen, sixteen days before her death, in a slanty and scratchy script that no longer sits on top of the lines of the pages but flows directly over them. In it she refers to the Estonian woman for whom she shops and cooks, and for whom she fights nursing home staff:

The situation with the Estonian keeps getting worse. I'm getting increasingly agitated and angry. Yesterday, in front of everybody, I lost my temper and bawled them out. I'm embarrassed by my behavior, but I could no longer control myself. I feel so sorry for her, and I can't seem to get her any help. Filled with shame and fear, I'm going to visit her today. (October 15, 1969, Diary 29)

In her penultimate diary, Šimaitė describes to what extent the Estonian has been neglected. After a prolonged illness, she has been left unbathed in bed for six weeks (April 10, 1969, Diary 28). The Estonian grows ever more childlike as her dementia progresses, and Šimaitė begins to despair at her own inability to elevate her friend's level of care (August 1, 1969, Diary 29). The Estonian woman does not speak, either in her own language or any other, but smiles at Šimaitė with thanks. Facial expressions are her only means of communication. In the end, the silent Estonian, who lives in a world inside her head, will survive Šimaitė.

Even on her deathbed, a caregiving habit retained a firm hold on Šimaitė. But of what was once a painful kind of joy ("My greatest happiness is that, despite my asthma, aching legs, general fatigue and weakness, I haven't forsaken the Estonian" [October 5, 1969, Diary 29]), soon only pain remains. Her final diary entry hints at the wound that both her altruistic behavior and continual letter writing may have concealed:

9. Šimaitė (right) at Cormeilles-en-Parisis, possibly with the Estonian woman.
Vilnius University Library Rare Books and Manuscripts Department.

JANUARY 1, 1970

*I think I've never had such a bad year. Last month was terrible. Illnesses,
and a harsh battle between life and death. . . .*

*And there's so much blood-drenched suffering everywhere in the world.
. . . And then my relatives. In the morning all I want is to sleep in. But I have
to get up, go out, help the Estonian woman. I won't abandon her. What sin
have I committed to have her sent to me here in Cormeilles?*

Psychologically and physically, I am totally exhausted.

And dirty. I can't even wash my hair or bathe.

*Christmas brought great joy — I got a lovely fir tree as a gift . . . lots
of candy, and I get an unending stream of letters and books. I don't even
know when I'll be able to say thank you. For some reason, an extraordinary
number of people thought of me this year.*

*Sometimes it takes me two or three days to write a single letter. And in the
meantime more and more obligations pile up. Sometimes one makes mistakes
trying to help. . . . And all this cuts me like a knife, tears my soul apart.*

Who will tell all those good people that I don't have the strength to write? *(Diary 29)*

In Šimaitė's mind, caring for her needy Estonian neighbor is transformed into a kind of penance. Similarly, it appears that her obsessive letter writing was some kind of penance for an unnamed past sin, the letters counted off like the beads of a rosary. Or perhaps the sin is not unnamed or unknown. Perhaps the sin and the penance are one and the same, two sides of the same coin. If the sin is writing too few letters, the penance is to write more; but writing letters is also a sin, since it is this kind of writing that precludes memoir writing. So Šimaitė is guilty whether or not she writes — either way, she is committing a sin. Although an atheist, here the vestiges of her Lithuanian Catholic roots are plain to see.

In her letters Šimaitė faulted her friend Kauneckas, the Translator, for his "dictionary mania." Wasn't she herself suffering from a mania, a "textual mania?" Her problem in not writing her memoirs was thus not writer's block, it was an excess of letter writing, a kind of letter-writing sickness — an epistolophilia — which precluded any other kind of writing. Such letter writing was a studied avoidance of the kind Sigmund Freud talks about when describing his patients who won't heal. In "Remembering, Repeating and Working-Through," Freud tries to account for the fact that some of his patients are getting worse with treatment. He describes their compulsive repetition of symptoms as replacing the impulse to remember. The compulsion to repeat gradually enters every activity and relationship in the patient's life, so that the symptoms of the illness (that is, whatever the patient repeats) eventually become a kind of ambivalent refuge:

His illness must no longer seem to him contemptible, but must become an enemy worthy of his mettle, a piece of his personality, which has solid ground for its existence and out of which things of value for his future life have to be derived. The way is thus paved from the beginning for a reconciliation with the repressed material which is coming to expression in his symptoms, while at the same time place is found for a tolerance for the state of being ill. (152–53)

In Šimaitė's case her compulsive letter writing might well displace or replace the remembering that writing a memoir would necessitate. After recording an interview about the "terrible times of the past" only six months before her death, Šimaitė wrote in her diary: "I would like to erase them from my memory. It would be better if it had all just been a dream, rather than reality" (June 22, 1969, Diary 28). Thus letter writing for her, as Freud rightly points out, is simultaneously a refuge and an enemy. Like any addiction, letter writing for Šimaitė represents both the poison and the medication that numbs the pain associated with it.

"You must tell your story," Šimaitė was told time and time again. It may have been too much to ask of her. "Who will tell all those good people that I don't have the strength to write?" she asked. The answer to this question lies with the researcher, the archivist, the young novelist — to all of whom, in different ways, she addressed her letters.

PART 2

CHAPTER 6

A Childhood Tale

ŠIMAITĖ spent her first eight years in the Lithuanian countryside where her grandparents raised her amongst its trees, lakes, gardens, and rivers. In the fields and forests she collected berries, mushrooms, and wove flower wreaths to wear on her head. At home she helped her grandmother tend the house and garden, and while they worked she listened to tales about undersea palaces, fairies, and deities. In Šimaitė's young mind the surrounding forest became populated with friendly spirits and talking animals.

Such is the idyllic childhood setting that Šimaitė described in a French composition. For years she took language lessons in Paris, and her notebooks bear standard teacherly comments about her grammar with no attention to content (Šimaitė's Papers, Vilnius University). But the story Šimaitė tells is a fascinating parable about the futility of vengeance.

After setting the scene, Šimaitė tells of her elderly aunt, who lived in her grandparents' house and liked to frighten her with cautionary tales of devils and how they punished disobedient children. Bad children went to hell, she warned. One night while in bed but not yet sleeping, Šimaitė was visited by a little devil.[1] Black as coal with big white eyes glittering in the darkness and turning its long red tail round and round in one hand, the creature struck her as cheerful and funny, not at all like the devils her aunt described. The next morning, hearing this, the aunt flew into a rage, spitting, "When you die, you are going to hell! You'll burn for eternity!" Šimaitė stood before the old woman silent and seething, wanting only to cause her pain.

In turn-of-the-century rural Lithuania it was traditional to buy one's own coffin and burial clothing. Every spring Šimaitė's aunt aired her funeral outfit, including a finely tailored blouse with the most beautiful buttons her niece had ever seen. She wanted the buttons desperately, imagined what they would look like on her dresses or how they would feel in her palm, but knew her aunt would never give them up. God himself would admire her buttons when she presented herself before Him in those clothes, the old woman used to say.

Returning from the forest, Šimaitė found the blouse with the beautiful buttons hanging to air. With no one around she took a kitchen knife and cut the buttons off the blouse in a swift motion, caught each one in her left palm, walked quickly to the river, and buried them in a sandy bend.

The theft had its desired effect. She returned home to find the old woman in tears. But Šimaitė felt only shame.

In concluding remarks she suggests a moral for the story: that revenge brings nothing. But perhaps her tale can be understood differently. Perhaps it can be read as a tale of preparation for death. The aunt, with her coffin and clothes, prepares each spring for Death's visit. In stealing the buttons, the little girl identifies what is beautiful and long-lasting. The fabrics will rot in the mossy earth of Lithuania, and the coffin too, but the buttons will last forever. In burying the brass buttons in the river bend, Šimaitė performs her first act as an archivist. Although she will never steal again, the knack for identifying the piece that matters, the thing that will endure, and the drive to protect it, will remain forever.

The work of an archivist is to prepare for death. Every record written, document filed, and book cataloged is a gift to the future — signposts to buttons buried in river bends. "What is written," as she once put it in a letter to the poet Kazys Boruta, "will never die" (April 12, 1934, Kazys Boruta's Papers, Mažvydas).

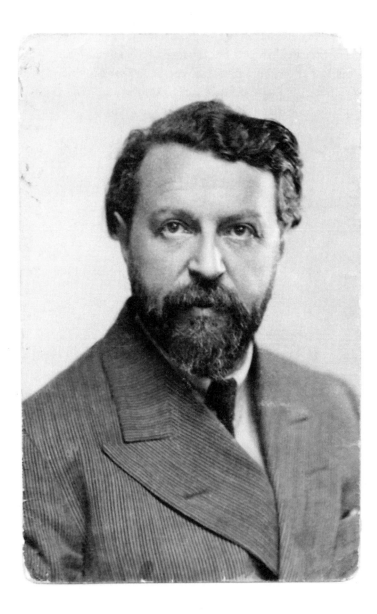

10. Isaac Nachman Steinberg, 1935. YIVO Archives.

CHAPTER 7

Russian Letters

ŠIMAITĖ'S silence about the ghetto and the camps in Lithuanian is only one part of the story of her writing. While she wrote very little on the subject in her native language, the situation changes dramatically in her Russian writings.

Immediately after the war, Šimaitė wrote a lot. From 1945 to 1947 she penned her promise-keeping letters. As soon as she was released from the last of the camps, she began to record her friends' stories and send these accounts out to friends and families of the dead. With each letter she kept a promise to someone who hadn't survived, someone who had asked her to pass on messages of love or simply of how they died. Then, after two years, she stopped. The silence extended to her Russian letters, and the ghetto and camps became as rarely mentioned there as was already the case elsewhere.

One Russian letter stands out for its length and detail. The eighty-eight-page typescript, bearing neither title nor salutation, is a letter to Isaac Nachman Steinberg (1888–1957), an author, Socialist Revolutionary, and the Commissar of Justice in the Soviet Coalition government of 1917 (Steinberg Papers). Its voice is remarkably literary, so that at first it seems to be a fragment of an autobiography or memoir. Not until page nineteen does Šimaitė use the second person, referring to "your book *Maria Spiridonova*," Steinberg's 1935 biography of the Russian revolutionary. Only here is the addressee revealed, and only here does it become clear that the text is a letter, written in Toulouse around October 1945 and sent to Steinberg in New York the same year. In a letter to Marc Dworzhetsky dated November 19, 1945, Šimaitė makes reference to a text about "Gershon Malakiewicz . . . and about other friends" (Dworzhetsky's Papers). She tells Dworzhetsky that it has already been translated into Yiddish and will appear in the publication *Oyfn Shvel* (On the Threshold). Like the other short texts Šimaitė wrote about the Vilna Ghetto, this text appears never to have been published in its original language.

Easily the most systematic piece of testimony she ever produced, the letter to Steinberg describes in detail her activities during the Nazi occupation of Vilnius. It tells how she gained access to the ghetto, how much institutional support she had from the university in her endeavors (quite a lot, as it turns out), whom she visited and what she saw, and how she spent her days running "errands" (her words) for both friends and strangers imprisoned behind its walls. The letter offers a rare glimpse of life outside the Vilna Ghetto, of relations there between Jews and non-Jews, and remembers individuals who would otherwise be erased from memory. It also gives us a glimpse of the workings of the Socialist Revolutionaries who, after having ended up on the wrong side of the revolution, had to flee the USSR, or die in its prisons, gulags, and purges. Finally, the letter touches on the Territorialist movement, known formally as the Freeland League, whose goal was "to find an unoccupied territory suitable for settlement by Jews who, for ideological or other reasons, did not wish to go to Palestine. The settlers' main occupation was to be agriculture, and the Freeland League established agricultural colonies in Eastern Europe to prepare future colonists" (D. Abramowicz, "My Father's" 21). Steinberg, a major proponent of the movement's ideology, traveled to Australia in 1939 to negotiate the establishment of an autonomous Jewish settlement in the Kimberleys of the northern region of Western Australia. By all accounts (including his own 1948 book, *Australia, the Unpromised*

Land), he might have succeeded in saving thousands of lives, had he been able to move through the Australian bureaucracy more swiftly. By the time an agreement seemed close, World War II was well underway.

Šimaitė received no payment for her actions, and was even uncomfortable with the idea of seeking compensation from the Germans after the war. In a July 7, 1957 diary entry she writes:

Everyone's after me to apply for compensation from Germany for the time I spent in the camps. They say that I'll get millions and my troubles will be over. Of course, this makes me laugh inside. No one is given money that easily, especially such large sums. And where is the ethical side of all of this? I will not allow anyone to pay me for what I did during Nazism. And I would be ashamed, I just couldn't ask for compensation for that. And to testify how the Nazis hit me, spat on me, broke my bones? No, I can't relive that by recounting it to strangers. And even if I decided to apply, how much would I really get for four months' suffering in the camps? (Diary 18)

Eventually Šimaitė's friends managed to convince her to look into compensation, and she found to her surprise that the process was dignified and orderly:

Apparently, in 1956 the Germans passed a law regulating compensation to those persecuted under Nazism on racial, political or humanitarian grounds. Such a truly democratic law is very comforting to see. I think it's the first of its kind. . . . Even though my friends are encouraging me, I still feel guilty asking for compensation, even though it's enshrined in the law. And Steinberg, my moral advisor, who would understand and counsel me is no longer. (August 12, 1958, Diary 19)

More than once Šimaitė addresses the suggestion that she accepted wartime payment for helping Jews in her letter to Steinberg, saying "Sadly, these people couldn't conceive of what it meant to feel humanity and comradery." First and foremost, this letter tells us, Šimaitė acted out of love for her friends in the ghetto: for Sonya and Faivush Trupianski, for Gershon Malakiewicz, for the Lichtenstein family, and others. In the first days of the Nazi occupation, we learn from this letter, Šimaitė was seized by depression and timidity. She dared not visit her closest friends and colleagues for fear of offending them. But loved ones gave her courage to extend herself in friendship, and Malakiewicz emboldened Šimaitė even more. It was at his insistence that she became a courier between the ghettos of Vilna and Kovno, carrying hundreds of letters and verbal messages from one to the other.

But why write all this to Steinberg? There is no evidence that they ever met, though they could have either in Moscow around 1917 or else in Paris in 1937. One reason for her choice of addressee may be that Šimaitė's common ideology with Steinberg made him an easy interlocutor. Šimaitė retained a belief in social revolution throughout her life. She did not need to temper her revolutionary vocabulary for Steinberg, nor enter into long explanations about the ins and outs of party meetings and activism. And why write all this in Russian, when she produced the vast majority of her correspondence and diaries in Lithuanian?

Šimaitė felt she had no right to tell the stories of the Vilna Ghetto publicly. She was also loathe to draw attention to her own heroism and survival and minimized their significance. Perhaps she had simply witnessed too many deaths and felt that the few she had saved were just a drop in the ocean. She only wrote for publication if asked specifically to do so (for Yiddish or Hebrew newspapers) or privately to members of a select community: survivors and those to whom the dead had asked her to write. To these people she wrote in Russian, a shared language perhaps without particular significance.

But, on the other hand, could her choice of language have meaning? There are, to be sure, signs of trauma here. The temporal shifts in her Steinberg letter are constant and peculiar. It moves between the past and the present continually, enacting a kind of narrative schism, an inability to integrate the 'then' with the 'now.' Shame — at her own relative security and at her compatriots' behavior and overwhelming indifference — returns as a constant theme. And while her pain at the loss of her friends is palpable, their deaths are reported almost in passing and euphemistically, if at all. One reason for Šimaitė's use of Russian here may lie in the difficulty that she found in telling this story, and in the way we all live the connection between language and experience. Is it possible that Šimaitė found a way to say the otherwise unsayable in what may have been for her a kind of neutral language? In a language useful for the simple fact that it was other than the one in which she thought, reasoned, and remembered?

Survivors have often testified in second and third languages, and even ones acquired after their camp and ghetto experiences. A number of examples of this can be seen (and heard) clearly in Claude Lanzmann's film *Shoah*, where interviews are conducted in Polish, French, English, and Hebrew, among other languages. Shoshana Felman and Dori Laub have suggested that these choices and movements between languages are not without significance. Witnessing in a foreign or new language, they tell us, may allow for a productive estrangement from past events, allowing one to say the unsayable and translate the untranslatable (Felman and Laub 212–13). By writing in Russian, had Šimaitė perhaps found a way to testify to that which *her* language could not witness? In Felman and Laub's terms, is this her attempt at witnessing without splitting?

And then there's the question of silence. Why did she stop writing about what she saw and did during the Nazi occupation? Survivor silence is well known. First- and second-generation Israelis often remark on how their parents and grandparents never spoke of that time. Many survivors arrived in Israel after the war, shook off Yiddish names, discarded the language, and set about making babies and building a life and a country in Hebrew. Had they never wanted to talk about what they lived through? It seems that Šimaitė's path was typical of many survivors, who by and large also fell silent after 1947. What was it about this year that made everyone stop talking and writing? Did they fall silent because they felt no one wanted to hear? Or because they had said what they had to say? Because they just wanted to move on? Or is there a timeline of trauma and testimony at work here, with silence hitting everyone simultaneously?

In Šimaitė's case, in addition to all these possibilities, there also seems to be some regret at having said too much. To Dworzhetsky she writes an apology in 1947 after Steinberg evidently translated and published excerpts of another letter without permission. "It didn't even enter my head that Steinberg would have published all this," she writes, trying to placate a friend who has for unknown reasons taken offence. "Can you forgive me? I feel terrible" (January 14, 1947, Dworzhetsky's Papers). The experience seems to have left her gunshy. More than anything she fears hurting others or causing her friends problems with Soviet authorities. In the same letter she writes, "I can't find a way to write about Boruta [the Lithuanian poet] and how he got a passport for Noemi from the Lithuanian partisans. You see, the Bolsheviks could make life difficult for him for that. [Steinberg] asked me about Boruta, but I never thought he would publish it. I hope that you understand how terrible I feel."

Feminist theorists tell us that women's writing is inherently collaborative. They emphasize the ways women's lives connect out to other lives, and how women tend to write their lives in terms of their relationships to others.[1] This is a good description of Šimaitė's corpus. She conceived of writing as a conversation with a reader and as an act of friendship. Though she called her diaries "conversations with herself," I wonder if, on some level, she wrote them as conversations with the future, with a reader who would arrive only years later. Someone like me.

CHAPTER 8

Everyday Writings

WHEN I told a librarian colleague of my plans to publish both translations of Šimaitė's writings as well as her story, he exclaimed, "Don't do that! There isn't enough there!" Then, several years later, now well into the project, I walked into the Yiddish Institute at Vilnius University for a meeting. A young woman who worked there smirked when I told her that I was writing about Ona Šimaitė, clearly thinking, *another hero-worshipper*. I stressed (though why I needed her approval, insecurity be damned, I still don't know) that I was interested in Šimaitė's whole life, beyond the ghetto and Dachau. "Of course you are," she scoffed gently as if to say, *Honey, there's nothing there*.

Šimaitė's writings are twofold: on the one hand they have been kept because of their "historical importance" — these are the writings of a woman who witnessed great and tragic world events, endured tortures, saved lives, and acted heroically. Her papers contain correspondence with a number of prominent intellectuals: Algirdas Greimas, Isaac Nachman Steinberg, Dina and Hirsz Abramowicz, Marc Dworzhetsky, to name a few; and her diaries describe meetings with the poet Abraham Sutzkever, writer Max Brod, and receptions by Israeli dignitaries including the President himself. But on the other hand Šimaitė's writings are ordinary, and carry all the signs of women's life-writing. They focus on the present, on the details and difficulties of everyday life, and mark time by tallying unending minute tasks like letter writing, floor washing, shopping, and sewing. Šimaitė is interesting both for how she is ordinary and atypical. She arrived in France just as the cult of domesticity was taking hold, and would have been very much outside of the norm of what a woman was supposed to be.

The Vichy regime had fostered a traditional view of woman exemplified by its slogan: *Travail, Famille, Patrie* (Work, Family, Homeland). A woman's place was in the home, at her husband's side, and serving her children. And with so many dead and deported, after the war pronatalist policies continued until the 1960s. France needed babies, and lots of them. Whether a woman should work, have control of her assets, control of her reproductive system, or receive equal pay for equal work, remained topics for discussion for decades after the war (in 1962 French women's salaries equaled only 64 per cent of the male average) (Duchen 159). But these questions would hardly have applied to Šimaitė's life. A single, childless woman was expected to work (in the 1950s there was a shortage of workers, not jobs) and control her own finances. Her reproductive status was moot, both because of her age and because the right to sexual satisfaction outside of marriage (or even within marriage) wouldn't come onto the table until the 1960s. In a place that constructed womanhood and femininity as primarily belonging to the domestic sphere, Šimaitė would have been something of a curiosity.

Pages and pages of diaries, letters, and notes. Heroic deeds, travels, tragedy, hardship, poverty. Revolution. Šimaitė's writing is both mundane and sophisticated. Flat and poetic. Tedious and enlightening. Just as the woman herself. There is a story here, anyone can see that. So why is it so hard to find?

I am not the first to try and write Šimaitė's story. Amongst her letters I found evidence of such an attempt from a woman called Roberta Goldstein (*Cry Before Dawn, Memories that Burn and Bless*), a poet who wanted to write a drama about the Vilna Ghetto and

about Šimaitė. She and Šimaitė carried on a complicated correspondence through translation. Goldstein would write to Šimaitė in
English, her letter would then be translated. Šimaitė would respond
in Russian, and in turn her text would have to be translated for
Goldstein. Eventually, for simplicity's sake, the two women began
corresponding in French.[1]

The poet Goldstein lived in Vermont. I imagine her surrounded
by lush mountains, trying to call to mind the narrow cobblestone
streets of Lithuania. In her letters to Šimaitė she laments her lack
of Yiddish:

*I realize that all details have been carefully and painstakingly recorded
and in visiting the archives and viewing the faded and poignant pictures I
have an empathy for the entire situation. However I would have to write
in a fictionalized vein and hence could not hail the heroes and heroines of
those grim days by exact name. Perhaps that would not be so important if
I write from the heart. (Goldstein in D. Abramowicz's Papers)*

A bibliographical search turns up nothing of this endeavor, so I can
only assume that her text remained unfinished.

Another attempt to write Šimaitė's story was made by a man
described to me as a Texas oil baron, and whose name I no longer
recall. In 2002 a Kent State University archivist allowed me to look
at a manuscript long ago submitted for publication and rejected. The
baron had spent years researching and writing his book. Mastering
none of the languages necessary to read Šimaitė's papers, he had
commissioned translations of the archival documents, and paid for
them out of pocket. What possessed him, a non-academic busi-
nessman, to undertake such a project, I don't know. But a single
rejection was too much to handle, and after the first press turned
him down, he didn't have the heart (or didn't know) to continue
searching for another venue.

What makes this story so alluring, yet unwritable? Is it that we
drown in the details? Is there simply too much? Too little? Too
little of too much, or the opposite?

11. Šimaitė (left) in Israel. Vilnius University Library Rare Books and Manuscripts Department.

Dailiness infuses Šimaitė's writing. In her journals she contrasts the minutiae of laundry, floor washing, shopping, dishes, doctor's visits, and letter writing with "living for herself": visiting museums, art galleries, cinemas, spending time with friends, and above all, reading. Fed up with a life of poverty and drudgery in Paris, the promise of a life-time pension and accommodation lured her to Israel, and in early December, 1953, Šimaitė departed by ship for "the land of her dreams."

But Israel dealt her a tough blow when life there turned out to be harder than in Paris. The diaries of those years reflect her struggle to accomplish mundane tasks and her difficulty in adapting to the climate and culture of the young country. After fleeing the dailiness of life in Paris, Šimaitė now found herself even more burdened by domestic details.

DECEMBER 13–14, 1954

Monday was an inhumanly difficult day, even in the concentration camps we didn't work that much. I woke up at 2:30 a.m. and worked until 4:00 to try

12. Šimaitė with the dolls she made. Vilnius University Library Rare Books and Manuscripts Department.

and catch up with some of my literary debts. Later I had to fix my dress and darn my stockings. From 7 until noon I prepared meals, did laundry, and washed the floor. My room was very dirty. After that I took around ten kilos of books to Eged and visited Anda in the hospital. She leaves for Holland the day after tomorrow, poor thing. May the operation be successful this time!

I spent Tuesday morning ironing and patching, and gathering odds and ends for my trip to the kibbutz. I only had two hours left for work. (Diary 6)

In writing Šimaitė's story, we have to account for the simultaneous largeness and smallness of her time on this earth. We need to reconcile her thoughts on anarchy and totalitarianism with poetic passages about her love for cats; cubism with doll-making; literature with laundry. The story of Šimaitė must rise to the challenge of dailiness.

Rather than giving me pause and making me wonder if I was trying to write the unwritable, evidence of previous failed attempts to tell Šimaitė's story spurred me on. I am not alone in my sense of responsibility to my subject. Like other women writing the stories of foremothers, I want to save my subject, preserve her traces, dignify her memory.[2] We who work on women's life-writing engage in a kind of archaeology. In the dailiness of diaries and letters we look for beauty, wisdom, for untold stories, and insight into a time, place, and a feminine way of life. And those of us who are literary scholars, rather than historians, look for literature. Our task is to read life-writing seriously, and as literary artifact.

Šimaitė's letters unfold against the backdrop of the historical events she witnessed: the Russian Revolution and Great Famine, mass Soviet deportations, ghettoization, Nazi concentration camps, post-Vichy reprisals in Southern France, the birth of Israel, and May 1968 in Paris. The thousands of pages of her writing combine traits of traditional autobiography and biography — with their interest in Great Men and their Great Works (here, a Great Woman who did Great Things) with the themes of work, relationships, dailiness, and non-linear time, so characteristic of women's life-writing and autobiography (Long 45–46). Passages outlining chores, musing on doll- and dressmaking, an accounting of letters written, packages sent, and films seen bury references to her arrest, torture, exile, and internment. The big and the small, the historical and mundane coexist in the life-writing corpus.

PART THREE

CHAPTER 9

Ghetto

THE period that set the course for Šimaitė's exile, caregiving, chronic pain, letter writing, and journaling began with the year 1940, when she arrived in Vilnius from Kaunas to work at the newly baptized Vilnius University, where Lithuanian now replaced Polish as the official language of instruction. Vilnius, a city long under dispute, had been seized from Poland by the USSR in 1939 and returned to Lithuania for strategic reasons. For some six months, Vilnius found itself in a state of limbo, the legal but not yet de facto capital of Lithuania.[1] Lithuanian citizens arrived in the city to take over positions in municipal and social institutions, but shortly thereafter, in June 1940, the Soviet army occupied the Baltic States, making Vilnius the capital of the Soviet Socialist Republic of Lithuania. The new regime abolished political parties, closed newspapers, and imposed ideological reforms in education.

Isolated from its neighbors by war, the city became an uncertain refuge for thousands of Jews and Poles. They arriving maimed by bombings or frostbite, having walked hundreds of icy kilometers to escape German occupation of neighboring Poland. Soup kitchens, schools, charities, and shelters popped up to accommodate them, but lice, hunger, and filth abounded despite the hospitality effort.

Between June 13 and 16, 1941, the Red Army forcibly removed some 17,000 people — teachers, politicians, military men, house-wives, and children — to the Siberian steppes. Those carrying out the orders called the deportees bandits, nationalists, and fascists, but most were ordinary people, guilty only of owning a business, possessing an education, or being in the wrong place at the wrong time. A significant proportion of the deportees were Jews — merchants and Bundists — whose fate would later be envied because Jewish deportees ultimately fared better than those left behind. And so, people of all walks of life — including my own paternal grandmother, a farmer's daughter and mother of three — were loaded into cattle cars and freight trains. No one was allowed to approach them to offer food, milk, or water, and sanitary conditions were deplorable as they traveled east for weeks. Some ended up in permafrost regions, others found themselves on arable land infested by legendary mosquitoes. They built, then worked collective farms for anywhere from three to seventeen years.

The deportations not only proved fateful for families who lost loved ones, but for setting the course of later events. Until then Lithuanian Jews had lived in relative peace with their neighbors, free of Polish- or Ukrainian-style pogroms. As the poet and now politician Emanuelis Zingeris has put it: "Before the war, the Jew was a part of the Lithuanian landscape: wherever you went, you would find a cow, a peasant, a horse, a Jew, and a bicycle," but the deportations ruptured the traditional co-existence (Emanuelis Zingeris qtd. in Karvelis 34). Some Lithuanians now accused their Jewish neighbors of welcoming the Soviets and taking an active role in the deportations. This, despite the fact that a higher proportion of the Jewish population was deported than of ethnic Lithuanians. Anti-Semitism was on the rise, especially among students, and the Siberian deportations tipped the scales. When the Red Army withdrew in the summer of 1941, nationalists took it upon themselves to start the Nazis' murderous work for them. The Lietūkis massacre, perpetrated in Kaunas before the arrival of the SS in that city, has come to represent the brutality of the interregnum (Šuras 24, Greenbaum 306–07).

On June 20, 1941, the Soviet Union dispatched freight trains to collect its citizens and mass flight began. By noon the next day, the bombing of Vilnius was underway. German aircraft targeted the Green Bridge fifty times, but failed to hit it, destroying surrounding houses instead. Four days later, on June 24, 1941, German troops entered Vilnius. Locals — anonymous Lithuanians — killed scores of Jews and true or suspected Bolsheviks in the courtyard of the massive sixteenth-century Franciscan Church, whose gray façade and red roof loom high on Kėdainių Street.

Gates and walls, some falling and covered in graffiti surround the former monastery. They extend a full block on each of its four sides, and it seems like I walk kilometers before I find a way in. I arrive just as mass is letting out. Incongruously, cars line the square in front of this centuries-old building. Like so many churches in Vilnius, this one too is crumbling, and I step carefully over a trench where red bricks have been removed and piled to one side. In an apparent attempt to beautify the space during renovations and with Christmas approaching, someone has placed potted plants here and there on the stacks. Inside, it's freezing and cavernous.

Normally I light a candle for my late father every time I come into a church, but here, for the first time, I can't. I cradle my pregnant belly, as if to shield my baby from the truths of this place. They say the Madonna here is miraculous, and has healing powers, but if that were true, how was all that happened possible?

The first one shot was a young Jewish woman, lured inside the church gates (where all the cars are now parked) with the promise of work. The next victims: twenty Red Army soldiers trying to flee the city. By the end of the day, the courtyard overflowed with corpses exposed to the summer heat, until the fire department arrived to hose them down and take them away.

Just a few streets away, and in the shadow of yet another church in this city full of steeples, Šimaitė was despairing in her damp

13. The Franciscan Church in Vilnius. Photo by the author.

14. Number 13 Savičiaus (left) in Vilnius, where Šimaitė and Čilvinaitė shared an apartment. Photo by the author.

second-floor apartment at Number 13 Savičiaus, a cobblestone lane of cheap buildings where the university housed its workers. There Šimaitė shared accommodation with Marijona Čilvinaitė, her colleague and later her correspondent. The two women had known each other already in prewar Kaunas where they worked together. Today the house is a honey-brown color with some graffiti on one corner and a surveillance camera perched up high. It is only four o'clock on a cold December afternoon, but already the sky is darkening, and the city seems to be winding down to a whisper. The two librarians weren't roommates for long. Čilvinaitė left the city for the relative safety of her ancestral home in the countryside. But her first letter to reach Šimaitė after the war offers a description of their experience of the Vilnius bombings in that second-floor apartment:

SEPTEMBER 14, 1957

Dear Ona,

We said goodbye to one another in the Vilnius flood of screaming bombs, people's tears, sorrow, and other horrors of war. Back then it seemed like nothing could bring us joy again, that our hearts would never again allow us to be happy, that art and flowers wouldn't inspire us anymore, to such an extent had the hell of war darkened everything.

I still remember how calm you were during the bombings. Overwhelmed with anxiety, I used to wake you up, pull you behind the cupboard and sit you down on a blanket. The terrifying howl of the airplanes drove me out of my skin . . . but you, exhausted by human suffering, would fall asleep once again, and even start to snore, which made me so angry.[2] After the war I heard how much you had suffered and I didn't think that there was any way you could have survived. (Šimaitė's Correspondence, Hoover)

In the first days of the German occupation, Šimaitė buried herself in handicrafts and library work. She dared not visit Jewish friends, imagining they hated her. But when her friend Gershon Malakiewicz appeared one day, he convinced her that now more than ever they needed her. Even before ghettoization she began extending herself in any way she could: finding storage for valuable objects that could later be sold, raising money to pay fines, escorting released Jews home from prison, trying to gather news of the disappeared, and disseminating information among the frightened Jewish community:

In addition to almost daily visits with friends, it was necessary to run errands for both comrades and various others. I had to look for people to help me. They were difficult to find. . . . It was necessary to procure food, money, to deliver these, to collect and sell remaining items, fetch documents, hide people, and so on. Each of us managed to accomplish these things and it would have been inconceivable to do it without relationships to, and advice and help from others. (Šimaitė in Šukys, "And I burned" 59–60)

In her Steinberg letter, Šimaitė describes how on September 6, 1941, "Jews were led like criminals into the ghetto at gunpoint" (Šimaitė in Šukys, *"And I burned"* 55). Out in the streets of Vilnius, she continues, men and women, the young and old, the healthy and

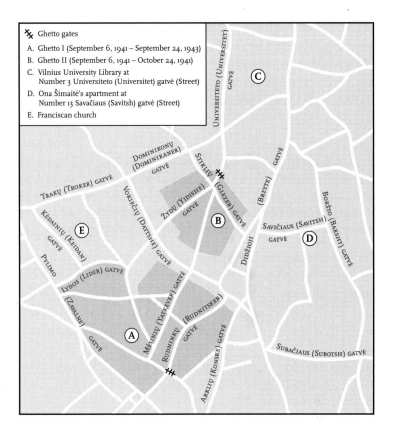

Ghetto gates

A. Ghetto I (September 6, 1941 – September 24, 1943)
B. Ghetto II (September 6, 1941 – October 24, 1941)
C. Vilnius University Library at
   Number 3 Universiteto (Universitet) gatvė (Street)
D. Ona Šimaitė's apartment at
   Number 13 Savačiaus (Savitsh) gatvė (Street)
E. Franciscan church

UNIVERSITETO (UNIVERSITET) GATVĖ

DOMINIKONŲ (DOMINIKANER) GATVĖ

STIKLIŲ (GIEZER) GATVĖ

BREITEJ GATVĖ

BOKŠTO (BAKSHT) GATVĖ

TRAKŲ (TROKER) GATVĖ

VOKIEČIŲ (DAITSHE) GATVĖ

ŽYDŲ (YIDISHE) GATVĖ

KĖDAINIŲ (KEIDAN) GATVĖ

SAVIČIAUS (SAVITSH) GATVĖ

DIDŽIOJI

PYLIMO

LYDOS (LIDER) GATVĖ

MĖSINIŲ (YATLEVER) GATVĖ

RUDNINKŲ (RUDNITSKER) GATVĖ

(ZAVALNE) GATVĖ

ARKLIŲ (KONSKE) GATVĖ

SUBAČIAUS (SUBOTSH) GATVĖ

2. The Vilna Ghetto and surrounding neighborhood. Street names appear in Lithuanian. Yiddish equivalents appear in parentheses.

the sick — some carried on stretchers — women with babes in arms, on their backs, or in carriages, converged in the old town from all parts of the city. The Germans put up a wooden wall around the narrow cobblestone streets and alleys, and soldiers drove terrified families with shouts to move faster. A few of the wretched, unable to carry on, threw their belongings to the ground, leaving the spoils for scavengers.

I saw how on this day a worker extended a hand to a Jew who was being led away in the convoy. They arrested the worker, despite his protests and explanations that this Jew was an old friend who had helped him a great deal in times of need. A Lithuanian soldier insisted on his arrest, and the worker was taken to the police station. (Šimaitė in Šukys, "And I burned" 56)

Onlookers crowded both sidewalks.

In the days following ghettoization, unable to visit her friends behind the walls and anxious for their health and safety, Šimaitė went out each afternoon to watch for work teams returning to the ghetto. She spotted Malakiewicz lugging a bag of firewood whose weight made the veins in his neck bulge. He came close enough to brush shoulders and pressed a few letters into her palm. The letters came from people who had arrived in the ghetto with nothing. Fearing their children would starve, women whose husbands had disappeared in previous weeks asked for food or money. "At 7:00 p.m. I [met] with Belochka Lichtenstein. She also [pressed] a letter into my hand: 'Anichka, help, I don't even have a husband. I have two small children and elderly parents'" (Šimaitė in Šukys, "And I burned" 59).

Eight days after the walls went up, Šimaitė visited the ghetto for the first time.

CHAPTER 10

Mowszowicz

WHEN I am not wandering the streets of Vilnius, I spend my days in the university's manuscript reading room, sifting through thousands of letters. All around students hunch over fragile Russian books and old Lithuanian texts. It is stuffy and smells of perspiration. The desks are small, and many of the power outlets don't work, so I have to tread carefully around the computer cords that snake from one station to another. There is far more material than expected, and I have to work hard to get through it all.

The Vilnius University librarians have received me with a touching kindness — women are in charge of almost every aspect of archival life here. They worry for me, these library women, offering pots of tea and scolding me when they think I have been sitting still for too long.

On the second or third day of my work at the library I notice a plaque that hangs on the back wall of the manuscript reading room. It reads:

Elena
Eimaitytė-Kačinskienė
1906–1989
Assistant to the Director of Vilnius University Library
(1940–1944)

I photograph it a few times, though in the low light of the room, the images come out blurry. Even so, these pictures serve as my first record of Elena Eimaitytė's existence outside of texts. Until now I have only known her name through Šimaitė's letters, so the plaque startles and reminds me that the story I am tracking is not a secret that I share only with Šimaitė.

In 1941 Eimaitytė was thirty-five years old. Like Šimaitė and Čilvinaitė, she arrived in Vilnius in January 1940 as a member of the staff whose task it was to reinvent the formerly Polish Stephen Batory University, transforming it into the Lithuanian institution of Vilnius University. In 1944 Eimaitytė left Lithuania for the United States, married a mathematician, and worked in a number of libraries, including the Library of Congress. I learned her name from Šimaitė's Steinberg letter:

In the middle of the first week of the ghetto's creation, the head secretary of Vilnius University library, Miss Eimaitytė, asked me if would like to go to the ghetto with Miss Godliauskaitė. I jumped at the offer. I myself had already been racking my brain on the subject, but hadn't been able to come up with any way to get through the security surrounding the ghetto to see those friends who didn't go out into the city to work.

Half an hour later, Miss Eimaitytė delivers to me an official document signed by the director of the university library and addressed to the head of the Office for Jewish Affairs, Mr. Burakas. The library requests him to permit me, as head of the cataloguing department, and Miss Godliauskaitė, as head of the reading room, to go into both ghettos with the purpose of collecting a few unreturned library books. I go to see Mr. Burakas alone. Without any discussion, he gives me a visa to both ghettos for September 14. (Šimaitė in Šukys, "And I burned" 60)

Despite its walls, the ghetto was porous. Each day groups of workers exited and returned through its main gate. Soldiers subjected prisoners to searches for food, weapons, documents, or even flowers smuggled under clothes. The discovery of food usually resulted in a public whipping, but for weapons, the punishment was death. Lithuanians sold chickens through holes in the ghetto wall to starving prisoners willing to pay inflated prices. At night, youngsters used a side gate on Mėsinių (Yatkever) Street to join the partisans in the forests.

The seven narrow cobblestone lanes of Ghetto I housed the lucky ones, deemed useful for their skills. Beyond the lanes' gateways lay courtyards and crowded apartments, barbershops, cafés, bath houses, schools, workshops, soup kitchens, and even a library. The ghetto teemed with life. Groups of children in need of stimulation inside the shrunken world interviewed their neighbors and set about writing a ghetto history, courtyard by courtyard.

Ghetto II imprisoned unskilled workers. Little more than a transit point for those condemned to immediate death, it barely lasted a month. In October 1941, the road from Ghetto II, or the Small Ghetto, as it was called, led to the pits of Paneriai (Ponar).

As I cross the former ghetto threshold, I study the buildings on each side of the street. To the right, a flower shop nestles between a café and strip club, and on the left, where more buildings once stood, there is now a park. Its trees sport red berries, and people huddle in threes and fours, drinking from large cans. A young man with his back to me takes a piss by a bush, and over all of this looms All Saints' Church, with its rose-colored towers.

Despite the shiny windows, life here is still hard for some people.

Winding my way down the lanes, I come across a Yiddish sign, a remnant of a prewar store, painted above an archway: a rare relic of Jewish life and the Yiddish language that flourished here when the magnificent Strashun Library still stood. The Germans pillaged and destroyed its contents, sending thousands of precious books to paper factories. Crumbling garages and fluttering laundry now clutter the courtyards that were the playing fields, marketplaces, social clubs, and execution grounds of the ghetto.

Early in the morning on September 1, 1941 the inhabitants of a building on Stiklių (Glezer) Street were ordered out of their apartments and into the courtyard. Lined up in two rows, the tenants were stripped of their keys by the building janitor, then taken to jail for two nights, before being ordered into waiting trucks and driven through a forest. The women and children left inside the vehicles listened as their men were shot outside, then they too were unloaded and made to wait at the edges of pits already piled with corpses.

The child who related this story returned from Paneriai alive, having been dragged out of a mass grave by a local woman. At first no one believed such witnesses, because the scenes they described were too terrible to imagine. A similar story was related by a girl from Strašūno (Strashun) Street taken away on September 2, 1941. She was shot in the arm then foot by a bullet that first passed through her mother. She and two others who survived the massacre were cared for by village women who lived near the killing site.

A woman calls down to me from a balcony and asks if she can help me find something. When I answer that I'm just looking around, she nods and tells me that tour buses often come through.

"Jews used to live here, you know."

"Yes, I know."

Šimaitė presented herself at the ghetto gate on the morning of September 14, 1941. With her she carried messages for delivery in the ghetto, prepared over successive restless nights. After the guards checked her document and allowed her to enter, a middle-aged man with a long, straight nose and a dark receding hairline gestured to her. Yankl Mowszowicz,[1] assistant professor of botany at Vilnius University, was waiting for her:

The first thing that strikes you when you cross the threshold of the ghetto is its terrible crowdedness. It's difficult to walk through the streets on a Sunday. We all keep bumping into one another. People mill aimlessly in the streets. But some of them have books in hand. I have the impression

that we've found ourselves in some kind of infernal madhouse. (Šimaitė in
Šukys, "And I burned" 60–61)

Mowszowicz steered her to a room so crammed with people that
she wondered how they slept. He explained: those who settled on
the floor had the privilege of lying down. Some slumbered upright
in couches or chairs, two stretched out on the table, and a little boy
bedded down on top of the room's only cupboard.

We go with the professor to see others. It's the same picture. Men and women,
young and old, healthy and sick, married and unmarried, educated and
illiterate, believers and atheists, people of the most varied appearances and
convictions all together. No one is allowed a minute to oneself. In that kind of
environment it is difficult to converse as we would like. Professor Mowszowicz
takes us to the hospital. Here we breathe a little more easily. The sight of
white hospital coats acts as a sedative, as does the fact that people are at
work. After a few minutes, Godliauskaitė leaves me to meet her friends. . . .
They bring an old man into the hospital completely covered in blood.
He is very close to death. After a minute, I ask without thinking, "Who
could have dared beat him like that, and why?" Dr. Salit answers: "You
still have to ask?"
At the hospital gates, Professor Mowszowicz and Godliauskaitė are
waiting. She has tears in her eyes and explains that she can't take any more,
and wants to go to the Small Ghetto immediately to see her friends, deliver
her messages, and head home.
In the Small Ghetto, each of us goes to see close friends, finding the same
crowded conditions and crush. (Šimaitė in Šukys, "And I burned" 61–62)

In Vilnius I search for other traces of the botanist. From Eglė, the
daughter of the poet, Kazys Boruta, I learn that Mowszowicz survived the war by hiding in a house not far from the Cathedral. She
shows me a book with his photograph. Mowszowicz wears academic
robes and a squarish hat upon his shaved head. The photograph
was taken in Łodz, where he resumed his academic career in the
late 1940s. After the war, most of the city's Poles were resettled in
the former eastern provinces of Prussia in northern and western

Poland. Stephen Batory University and its Polish faculty relocated to the city of Torun (Briedis 229). At the Lithuanian State Archive I find Mowszowicz's personnel file from Vilnius University. Inside are another photograph taken shortly before the German occupation, a short autobiography, and curriculum vitae. This man, whose CV lists over fifty scientific articles, feared being unemployed in the ghetto. As Šimaitė wrote to Steinberg:

The unemployed have no right to exist. He would like to get even the most menial job at the university. He is anxious about the fate of his manuscripts. He asks me to find someone who could hide him. He wants to obtain illegal documents and poison, so as not to give the executioners the chance to do away with him. (Šimaitė in Šukys, "And I burned" 65)

In his letters to Šimaitė, Mowszowicz painted ghetto life in vivid detail, describing its rules, regulations, and leaders, as well as its baths, soup kitchens, sports fields, schools, and music conservatory. He wrote about the ghetto courts (prisoners judged a number of murder trials there, and condemned the accused to death on at least one occasion), its concerts, plays, and cultural exhibitions. He told of evenings when scholars gathered to share their writings and research, and how the ghetto children studied with enthusiasm and runny noses in their unheated and makeshift facilities. He chronicled the literary debates, holiday celebrations, the publication of the ghetto newspaper, the functioning of carpentry workshops and other trade schools, and the celebration to mark the lending of the 100,000th book from the ghetto library. Mowszowicz encouraged Šimaitė to write a text called "Inside the Ghetto and Beyond its Walls," stressing that she had to record her experiences. In her responses Šimaitė protested that she had no time to write, and that it was more important to give her time to the living than to dead texts.

After the death of her close friend, the opera singer Liuba Levitska (in whose "little ghetto cage," she would often spend the night after a concert or play), Šimaitė received a letter in which Mowszowicz called her a saint. Šimaitė replied angrily that she was no saint, but a sinner, who hadn't avenged Levitska's death by killing her tormentors. "What kind of a friend stands idly by in the face of a loved one's brutal murder?" she scrawled, her script shaky with rage. But Mowszowicz was always calm, gentle, and disarming in his generosity and concern for Šimaitė's well-being. "Are you well, do you have enough to eat?" he always asked. "How are you holding up? What can I do to help?"

Work, food, refuge outside the ghetto, forged documents, and poison were the wishes of the majority of Šimaitė's correspondents. "Later, one more terrible wish was added — to make it to the partisans in the forest, not to save one's life, but for the battle, having killed at least one enemy, weapon in hand. Even if they don't make it to the forest, many want to have guns so they can resort to them at the decisive moment" (Šimaitė in Šukys, "*And I burned*" 65).

Šimaitė received letters each time she visited the ghetto, and their content became increasingly varied over time. At first she destroyed the letters she received: notes asking for food, money, medicine, or for her to retrieve or sell items left outside the ghetto; appeals for medical books, books on the construction of houses and stoves, heating and lighting. She also destroyed the requests for music books, scores, and fiction she deemed too dangerous to keep at home. Later she found a number of good hiding places for the most interesting letters. The last of her caches was under a stairwell at the Vilnius University Library, where she hid two hundred and thirty letters: two hundred from the ghetto, and thirty from people in hiding after liquidation.

Letters that told of the fear of death she found the most difficult to answer. "I would like just one thing," read one letter, "to be allowed to sleep calmly through one night, and to be absolutely sure that no one will come for me. Neither for me nor for anyone else" (Šimaitė in Stankevičius 54). Šimaitė sometimes sat before blank pages for hours until a few words of comfort finally came to her.

In her responses, she wrote of the obligation to persevere, to work, and not to lose hope. But even as she put words to paper, part of her wanted to be honest and to say that there was no way out. Instead, she reminded her correspondents that Socrates continued to work until the very last minute. No one ever asked how she would behave in similar circumstances, she wrote in her letter to Steinberg, and she was grateful for it.

None of the ghetto letters that Šimaitė hid in her apartment or at the university library survived. After her 1944 arrest, German soldiers ransacked her apartment, and all the notes, letters, and manuscripts she was hiding disappeared. When in 1957 Šimaitė sent Čilvinaitė to search the library, she was of course devastated to learn that her friend had found nothing. We know something of the content of those letters only through Šimaitė's accounts.

Why did she risk her life to help others? Years ago in Jerusalem, I sat listening to a roomful of historians discuss this very question. The general consensus was that the motivation was simple: money. Gentiles helped Jews, the historians argued, because they profited by doing so. The discussion left me profoundly saddened. Nothing I have read by or about Šimaitė suggests that she acted out of greed, or that she made any material gains from her wartime activities. In fact, the opposite was true.

Šimaitė believed that the world could be a better place, that it could be more just. Before the war, she had ties to the Leftist Socialist Revolutionaries, an illegal party in interwar Lithuania, and though Šimaitė sometimes attended their secret meetings, according to her nephew, she was never a member of any party. One thing is clear: Šimaitė was no Bolshevik. Like Steinberg, her dear friend Malakiewicz, and other refugees from Russia, she too had ended up on the wrong side of the revolution.

Her diaries record that she had little patience for government and bureaucracy, which she condemned with colorful formulations, including the April 2, 1958 entry: "May the leaders of all states and administrations be damned. With his dramas about kings and run-ins with the leaders of institutions, like it or not, Shakespeare will turn you into an anarchist. There's no need to read a single ideologue's work" (Diary 19). As late as nine months before her death, she wrote again in her diary "Like it or not, I'm still becoming an anarchist" (April 10, 1969, Diary 28). Šimaitė was becoming (always in process, it seems) an anarchist in the sense — some might say the true sense — that she believed above all in individual responsibility, in doing what one could to help the weak, and in taking care of oneself whenever possible.

Many of her friends were imprisoned in the 1920s and '30s for their underground political activity and writings, so Šimaitė supported them by sending letters and books to them in prison.[2] To the imprisoned poet, Kazys Jakubėnas, she sent a tome of Pushkin's stories in Russian. In his letter of thanks he admitted that the stories bored him, but promised nevertheless to use the book to improve his Russian. True to his word, Jakubėnas eventually published translations of Nekrasov, Lermontov, and Esenin, and although he never became a fan of Pushkin, he and Šimaitė became fast friends.

15. Kazys Jakubėnas. F143-36 Mažvydas National Library of Lithuania Rare Books and Manuscripts Department.

CHAPTER 11

Letters to Kazys Jakubėnas, 1941–1943

OCTOBER 21 [1941, VILNIUS]

My dear, sweet Kazys! I got your letter and the French books a very long time ago. Thank you for everything. It's been a long time since I've written to you. But I never forgot you. I know that you are alive. And, in truth, there was never any time to write letters, even though I was getting up at 4 a.m. and going to bed at 8 or 9 p.m. Only Sundays were left. But even all of them didn't belong to me. Now that my left leg has swollen up and I'm forced to lie in bed, I will write letters to all my friends and read a few much-anticipated books. Otherwise, since the beginning of the war I've only read Feuchtwanger's "Jew Süss," "Josephus," and Werfel's "Musa Dagh."

Now, when I need healthy legs more than ever, isn't it maddening that I'm forced to lie in bed. . . .

Since my last letter, I've seen and experienced an enormous amount. People's brutal origins overpower their humanity. On September 1st I paid 1,500 rubles to get an elderly man out of jail. And even on that day, while I was waiting for him, thousands more Jews were being led to prison. I'll never forget it until the day I die. Today I got news that the old man has disappeared once more. I'll probably never see him again.[1] One after another, my closest confidants are dying. I'm ashamed to be alive, ashamed to have a roof over my head, ashamed to have the possibility of bathing, and so on, when thousands of people don't even have these basic things anymore, but when Damocles' sword is hanging over their heads at every hour, and when whoever feels like it can mock and torture them. If before now I simply loved them, then I now worship them and that endless suffering, because, in truth, only the chosen people can suffer that way. And how differently different people experience this.

Otherwise, I have no intellectual life. I barely manage to clean up after myself and bathe. All aspects of life are incredibly difficult now. I'm not studying any languages at all. It often happens with languages in my life that the circumstances become such that, even with the best will and intentions, there is no possibility of studying. It's painful with regard to French. On Sundays I go to the symphony. But I can't feel joy for anything with my entire soul like before. Every joy is poisoned, and I would so much like to feel joy.

A ghetto has been set up in Vilnius too. And on September 7th everyone was herded there in a single day. They were only allowed to take with them what they could carry. And on September 8th, even though it was a Sunday, fences were hurriedly nailed together during the day, so as to separate those who had been brought in from the Aryans. And yesterday the second ghetto was liquidated, and I don't know where those people went.

I'm really afraid of winter, because it will be a hungry and cold one. Even now I only eat like a normal person twice a week, when I get 200g. of butter and 350g. of meat. Otherwise it's just bread and potatoes. But this is already the third day that potatoes are nowhere to be found. Brutality and lethargy. Almost no cultural life left.

MARCH 7 [1942]

Dear Kazys! I received everything that you sent through Vitas. Thank you very much. It made me extremely happy to receive your letter and the new poems. They express the sentiments of our times so well. Write more of them, dear Kazys. I will await at least a few of the poems you've published for children, and later — a collection.

Delivering the money, Vitas tells me that you've said to use it only for myself. I don't really listen to those kinds of things when kind Bronička says them to me. But your wish will be fulfilled 100% immediately. I bought some soap and I want to have my teeth fixed. Without your support, this last thing would have been completely impossible for me.

I'm living much better this year than last. I'm not cold, because Jonas provided me with coal. It's terrible just to remember how I froze last year right up until the New Year. And the food situation isn't even as bad as last year, when there were days when there was neither bread nor potatoes, and I had to make do with salted coffee. It isn't like that now. The bread I get with my ration cards is enough for me, and I buy potatoes at free-market prices. This year I even have a steady supply of lard. Whenever I finish one piece of lard, more appears as if falling from the sky. And this happens without any requests on my part. Even these days there are still people who think about others.

But what I lack most is time, and I don't have any strength or health left in me, while there's so much that I want and need to do. I'd like to be able to live a little more normally. To have not only responsibilities but some free time for myself as well. I know that I'll only live once in this world, which is why I so much want to live for myself a little. If only I could get a good night's sleep, and then read and read. I want that so much! But when I'm confronted with the hellish sufferings of others, the desire to live for myself disappears. It seems that I'll never again know how to feel joy with my entire soul the way I used to. It's hard for me to keep believing that "Oh the mad times shall pass, oh the autumn will pass." . . . It seems that it will continue to get worse and worse.

I'm luckier than you in one respect. My trudgings don't always end in failure. Sometimes there are successes, however each of them, even the smallest, is bought for too high a price in energy and time. Just as the stars light up the proverbial night, each encounter through letters that we have with people who have a heart and a brain makes life brighter and easier. And there really are good people in the world. And endlessly brave and self-sacrificing ones. In this respect, life is really spoiling me. I have met so many good and interesting people. I'm very grateful to fate that I have you, dear Kazys, among my closest friends. I really wish that your life were easier, and that those people closest to you did not suffer.

Even if you were a Christian, I wouldn't want you to wish me entrance into heaven, when such a horrible hell is boiling on earth. Once there is heaven on earth, then there will be heaven in the soul and everywhere. Can anyone be happy when others suffer like this?

Lately life has been taking away everything that is so dear to me. A long time ago someone stole my "Songs of Suffering." All my efforts to find them have been fruitless. I miss them so much. Maybe you have a leftover copy? And even if you did, would you give it to me? Most likely you don't.

Well, take care. I kiss you. Best wishes to the friends, especially to Mečys. How is he? And Antanas and the others? Be so good as to write me a few words from time to time.

    Ona

APRIL 12 [1942]

Dear Kazys! it's rare that you spoil me with letters, but when I get one — it's a real celebration.

On the subject of paying you back, I could give you 10 rubles a month without much hardship. This wouldn't burden me at all. Thank you so much again for the help you've given me. How enormously I was in need of that money then! Alas, you're wrong when you write that for once you could help me. This wasn't the first time. In this respect you have a very short memory.

[page missing]

painful experiences already. Perhaps later, when these will no longer be experiences, but only chilling memories. And every day there's something new, and even more brutal.

It's good to know that you're not suffering from hunger, and that you still have some tobacco, even though I'm a strict enemy of smoking. There are days here when I eat well, but there are more days when I have to make do with only bread and water. But this doesn't matter to me, and I don't bother my head about it. The hardest thing for me is the cold and the filth. I haven't yet even been able to get soap, even for money. Even though I paid for firewood and I have a ration card, I never receive any, because people say that trees are still growing in the forest. I still have enough firewood for about one more week. With all the deductions my salary is 85 rubles. That would be enough if there weren't such a need to deal with the black market. And I don't even know what kinds of sums would be necessary to satisfy the most basic needs like soap and firewood. Every ten days I buy some meat on the black market.

At work, lists of Jewish authors whose books will be taken out of the libraries are hurriedly being prepared. Also to be taken out, without exception, are Soviet books and those by progressive Lithuanian authors. Sadly, never before have people read Jewish writers as they do now. It's a shame that they didn't do this earlier and that they didn't get to know this rich literature. Those who know anything at all about that literature are now constantly expected to hand over information about it. As people get to know this people's literature, they marvel at its richness and beauty.

A few days ago Jews were forbidden to give birth. Now the children who are born have to be killed, and women who become pregnant must have operations.

I went to a closed concert.[2] If we meet sometime, I'll tell you about it. I miss you terribly. But there's no point even thinking about our meeting. If you go to the country, let me know your address there. Take care. I squeeze your right hand.

     Ona

Dear, sweet Kazys!
I miss you very, very much. But it seems that there's no hope of our seeing each other. Occasionally I see you in a dream. I wonder if you are still in Kaunas, or if you have gone out to the province? Did you get the letter I wrote you before Kazys's [Boruta's] departure?[3] Well, Kazys is a pig's leg for not having brought me the manuscript. I asked him and you reminded him; he told me that you did. Maybe you can give it to Pranas to bring it.

    After Kazys's return I kept meaning to write to you, but I never got down to it: either I don't have enough time, or I'm very tired.

    Write me a few words at least. I'm happy that you did what Kazys has been telling me about.

    Work really doesn't provide anyone with anything right now: neither food nor clothes nor shoes. I work 8½ hours, and only earn two kilograms of bacon in total. But you have to search for it like some kind of hidden treasure or rarity. Because I give away half my salary, I'm only left with one kilogram of bacon. But this giving away of half of my salary lends a little bit of meaning to my work. And work is now boring and uninteresting. And it's inhumanly cold both at the office and at home. But I do heat my home once a week. We already start work at 7 a.m. I return from work at 4 o'clock, so tired that I don't even have the strength to write letters anymore: I lie down and read. And that's when I forget my fatigue and hunger, and everything. Over 9 whole months I can say that I've hardly read anything. Now I read a lot, because I go walking on those people's errands only when I work in the morning. After work I don't have the strength to take on any walks. I would very much like to start studying French again because I've forgotten almost everything, but since life is very difficult and cruel, it's not always possible to find the strength to concentrate and learn a foreign language. It's a different thing when you read a good book; then you forget everything.

    And it's such a cold spring this year. Even so, the trees and orchards are green, which gives me so much beautiful and quiet joy. The flowers are blooming as well, even if they're late. But I don't have very many spring flowers, since they're very expensive this year. How wonderful that there are good books and flowers in the world. Otherwise, I almost never meet up with anyone, only when I have business with them, because I'm either reading or out walking or I'm at work. I still go to concerts on Sundays.

How is life treating you now? What are you thinking of doing? Write me.

I squeeze your hand firmly. I wish you as much good as is possible right now. Unfortunately, I won't write about what is most on my mind.

Well, take care and be strong.

Ona.

SEPTEMBER 8 [1942]

Dear, sweet Kazys! Two weeks ago I got your letter, which made me very happy. Thank you, Kazys, for not forgetting me. True, your letter was gloomy, as the autumn days are gloomy. But how is a letter supposed to be sunny when life is so inhumanly difficult and cruel? I'm blessed with the lights of very interesting and good books and people — I'm luckier than you. But I don't have any time at all to benefit from this bounty, especially not to meet and have friendly conversations with people, when there's no business at hand. I so long for that. It's very rare that I have a casual heartfelt conversation. Aside from time, I'm very short of money, food, and especially coal. I can bear the shortages of food and money quite easily. The worst is not having enough coal. I shudder just at the thought that I'll have to live for 6 months — November–April — in an unheated room. My room is very cold and smells of mildew now already. Even now it's too cold to sleep with only the cotton blanket. In addition to that I cover myself with my winter coat, fall jacket, and I wrap my head in a woolen scarf. Covered like this I warm up, it's good. I even dream beautiful dreams in which I'm eating ham and cake. I don't know why I dream so often of these things, since even in better days I didn't eat them very much. One time, like in a story, I dreamed that my room filled up with little boxes that were made of biscuits. As soon as I started to want to eat them, I woke up. By morning I've warmed up and once I've woken up at 3 or 3:30 a.m. I mend my clothes (as if it's a prayer that I'm compelled to complete every morning), then read and write until 7 or 6. I have a great many books both from the library and from Felna, and I get some pretty good Latvian ones. When I compare the Latvian books, I become embarrassed for ours. There they publish many and quite good Latvian ones, not the garbage that we get here. A good book gives me an incredible amount of solace in these especially difficult times. You think; sometimes you argue with the author you've just read; you dream and then forget life's hardships.

Other people's troubles, suffering, and humiliations weigh heavily on my heart. But there's no way to help, even if you were willing to give your life. I suffer from the cold (there's no heat at all at the office either); but when I go where there are little children and the room is unheated, I not only feel cold, but my soul begins to suffer as well. One Lithuanian Vilnius newspaper is giving tips on how to protect oneself against typhus. But when there is no firewood or soap, those tips won't really help. I'm really suffering from the fact that I can't wash, bathe or do my laundry properly, because there are no bath houses, and firewood is incredibly expensive. We used to get tea at work, but not anymore. So every morning I have to make do with cold coffee and bread, I only have the opportunity to boil myself some . . . coffee and potatoes for lunch. As for eating, I eat every day, for I have potatoes. But to boil potatoes and coffee one has to use up 12 rubles' worth of firewood. The food doesn't vary from day to day — bread (though sometimes I'm short of it) and potatoes. A "party" happens only every two weeks when I get some butter and sugar. I'm starting to forget what meat looks like. There are huge lines in front of the butchers starting at 4 o'clock in the morning, and only the first ones in line are lucky enough to get a small amount (about 50–60 people at each butcher shop). We haven't had any barley for a long time now. In the last month we didn't receive any flour either.

I work from 9 o'clock in the morning to 7 o'clock in the evening with a lunch break. I don't like this work schedule at all. You can even do less for yourself than if you worked 8½ hours in a row, and it's more tiring. When I come home from work, I go straight to bed, because I'm so cold and tired. But early in the morning I feel good again. The symphony concerts used to give me the biggest pleasure, but because of the firewood shortage and the absurdity of life, there haven't been any for two weeks. If only there were one today! I go to the theater very rarely, because I don't have a lot of time, and the tickets are extremely expensive. In Riga it's a different situation. There, where prices are concerned, a working person has access to the theater. I went to the premier of Ibsen's "Nora." I liked it. Kazys [Boruta] was working with the artists during their rehearsals and was impressed with the theater's work. I'm very happy about that. Otherwise, Kazys is no longer in control of his nerves at all. It's sad just to look at him. But where will he find another person like Ona [Kazanskaitė-Borutienė], who would give herself to him and take care of him like that? And he needs someone; he doesn't know how to take care of himself. Kazys took an extraordinarily beautiful wreath to Ona's grave. I was at the cemetery that day as well with a colleague from work. *I've never seen such artistic wreaths anywhere as those in Vilnius this year. It would be worth writing an entire monograph about them. We didn't work the day of September 2nd. So, after visiting Ona's grave, I went to the Jewish cemetery. I walked around there for about 4 hours. The monuments are smashed; the headstones are knocked over or smashed to bits; there are huge piles of shit on some of the headstones, which probably means that the toilet in the cemetery is smashed as well; the rooms in which religious ceremonies are held are also smashed; photographs are shaved out of headstones or defaced. Of course, one, two, or even 10 people didn't do all this, because they wouldn't be capable of it even if they wanted to, but . . .*[4]

I read Mazalaitė's book "The King's Fire." What a bourgeois book that's of no use to anybody. Why didn't Kruminas advise her? I'm embarrassed for such a book. Best wishes to your brother and [the rest is written up the margin of the letter, and is illegible].

The last letter to Kazys is dated September 10, 1943, almost eight months before Šimaitė's arrest:

My dear, good Kazys! It's been three weeks since my return. Thank you for the day that we spent together. It's a great pleasure to remember it. I wanted to write to you earlier, but I'm so inhumanly pressed for time. The long hours at work, together with errands — mine and not mine — are knocking me off my feet. In this short period since my return, I've witnessed terrible things. And all this leaves a kind of heavy, heavy sediment in my soul.

I've started making notes. I didn't think that I'd have so much material. More and more new facts emerge from my memory. But there's so little time for notes and reading, because my job and the endless walking swallow up everything. And life keeps getting more difficult, for new shortages keep popping up. But even that would be nothing, if I only had more time and if I didn't see this kind of endless human suffering.

Though Šimaitė's and Jakubėnas's wartime letters are some of the most intimate of the entire corpus, I have no evidence that the two were lovers. Šimaitė's nephew confirmed that some people believe that they had become more than friends, but that war and political action likely precluded a romantic relationship. He told me too that she had once fallen in love with a Russian poet, and when she worked up the courage to declare herself to him, the man cruelly rejected her by postcard, mocking her appearance and surely leaving her more guarded with her affections. But her letters to Kazys are full of love, and I can only imagine the ones he wrote in return were the same.

Perhaps Kęstutis is wrong in believing their relationship remained platonic. A part of me hopes so.

CHAPTER 12

Destruction of the Ghetto

THE destruction of the Vilna Ghetto was rapid and dizzying. No one knew what to think when mass deportations of ghetto prisoners to Estonia began in August 1943. Many in the ghetto believed it was simply a matter of waiting out the war, and remaining alive long enough to see Hitler's defeat. If they could work in Estonia for a few months, they might just survive. When they arrived there, the prisoners cleared forests and experienced a strange sense of hope and doom. Every day the prisoners of the Estonian camps felt more and more hemmed in by the sky and vast forests around them. Even the sea in which they bathed every day — a pleasure they had almost forgotten in the Vilna Ghetto — was a bittersweet presence, demarcating the limits of where they could flee, if they ever got the chance.

Few of these deportees survived to see the end of the war. On September 18, 1944 the work camp inmates of Klooga and Lagedi, many of whom came from the Vilna Ghetto, were ordered to build a pyre, then to lie down naked on the logs, where one by one they were shot in the neck. The living layered upon the murdered, and the whole human structure was burned. The next morning the Red Army reached the area.

On September 23, 1943 the Gestapo liquidated the Vilna Ghetto and shot its remaining prisoners. The only Jews who now officially remained in Vilna were at two work camps outside the ghetto.

As rumors about impending liquidation circulated in the fall of 1943, Šimaitė secreted Sala Vaksman, a university student, out of the ghetto, either carrying her in a sack (as Vaksman's son in Israel told me) or disguising her in a long coat (as I read in Vaksman's testimony pages at Yad Vashem) and speaking loudly in Lithuanian (Šimaitė's Papers, Righteous File). The soldiers at the gate assumed that Šimaitė's companion was a colleague from the library, and let them exit the ghetto. First Šimaitė hid her friend in her Vilnius apartment, where Vaksman recovered from a fever for three weeks, then in a cupboard in the university's library. For months she spent her days inside the cramped piece of furniture; during the night, she stretched out on the long tables to sleep. One night in April 1944, Vaksman was discovered by two thieves, who had probably broken into the library looking for material to burn, since wood and coal were at such a premium. The library was no longer safe, so Šimaitė arranged a place for the student at Kailis (Fur), the work camp outside the ghetto walls, where prisoners made warm clothes for German troops.

A few days later, on April 28, 1944, the Gestapo arrested Šimaitė. Either her luck had run out, or (as she believed), someone had betrayed her, but in any case, the authorities discovered that she had provided a child with a forged identity document to get her into an orphanage.[1] Soldiers seized her, then ransacked her apartment. The notes, manuscripts, and printed texts Šimaitė had been hiding perished in the search. The Gestapo held her for twelve days. They hung her upside down during her interrogation, beat her, and burned the soles of her feet with hot irons. The Germans condemned her to death, but the university rector, Mykolas Biržiška, managed to raise enough money to pay a ransom for her life.

Instead of the gallows, Šimaitė was sentenced to imprisonment at Dachau. When they heard of her fate, university friends gathered warm clothes and sent a librarian to deliver them to her in prison. The colleague found Šimaitė only half-conscious, her wrists bandaged following an apparent suicide attempt.

Until May 1944 the Germans held Šimaitė in a forced labor camp called Pravieniškės, twenty-nine kilometers east of Kaunas. We know nothing of her internment at the camp, except that Jakubėnas snuck in to visit her. In her unfinished memoir about him, Šimaitė wrote:

I panicked when I realized that he had crossed into the restricted area. The Germans gave every brave soul caught committing such a "crime" two weeks in a labor camp where they would be humiliated and severely beaten. Luckily, they never caught Kazys. (Memoir about Kazys Jakubėnas, Šimaitė's Papers, Vilnius University)

From Pravieniškės, Dachau was the next stop.

The Germany-bound train sat in Kaunas for many hours. People approached Šimaitė's car, and offered to deliver news of her deportation to friends and family. But as her nephew explained to me over tea and vodka in Vilnius, Šimaitė had trained herself to forget names and addresses as soon as she delivered people to safety. She had confused her memory so much that she could no longer recall the names and addresses of loved ones in Kaunas. The train departed, and she left no messages to deliver on her behalf.

I think that Šimaitė spent around four weeks in Dachau, but I can only estimate, since I have found no official records. So rarely does she speak of Dachau that some Lithuanian journalists have suggested that Šimaitė never actually spent any time there. But her nephew rejects this suggestion, citing a postcard she sent to her friend, the Translator, Vytautas Kauneckas, from the camp during a 1960 return there. The card's short message describes her state of mind: "Today I'm at Dachau. I had to come here to cry it out of my system, and I've never prayed as hard as I did today. . . . It's difficult to write. I'm still breathing in tears and blood" (September, 30, 1960, in Šimas 59).

Šimaitė's 1960 diary attests that Šimaitė did, in fact, make a trip to Germany in July of that year. In an October 2, 1960, entry, she mentions Dachau specifically: "So much time has passed, and I still haven't had the chance to converse with myself. I went back to Germany, Obermergen, Dachau, Munich. So many impressions. I experienced many and suffered many things during that time. I'm often ill" (Diary 24). Four months after the trip to Dachau, she again defers writing about it:

NOVEMBER 22, 1960

I wrote those dearest to me about my trip back. Now I have to record it in my memoir notes as well. I'll leave Dachau for another time. I want to record this for myself in much more detail than in those letters. Today I have to hurry to complete other writings, and very painful ones, particularly those regarding Aldutė's wounds, so I have to defer my memoirs. There's no other choice. (Diary 24)

Whether or not she ever returned to the subject of Dachau, I don't know. There is no such text among her papers.

From Dachau the Germans transferred Šimaitė to a small camp in a village called Ludelange in occupied Lorraine, whose military barracks served as a prison for Russians. How or why they transferred Šimaitė isn't clear. Her nephew told me that they did this because she was ill. Another story is that the camp was full, so they moved out non-Jewish prisoners like Šimaitė to make room for those whom an even more terrible fate awaited.

PART FOUR

CHAPTER 13

Kazys

IN the final months of the German occupation Kazys Jakubėnas wrote a poem called "Paukšteliui" (For Little Bird) for Šimaitė. It begins:

Will you fly to her, dear little bird,
Beneath my beloved's little window?
Will you comfort her with your hymns
And your sweet, resounding voice?

Tell her that I'm alive and well,
The terrible days are far behind
(qtd. in A. Jakubėnas 18–19)

The poem turned out to be fateful for Jakubėnas. In 1946 Soviet secret police searched his apartment, taking away two suitcases filled with manuscripts, and charged him with counter-revolutionary activity under article 58, section 1 of the Soviet criminal code. He spent the fall, winter, and spring of 1944 imprisoned in a Vilnius cell, half underground.

Each night, agents interrogated him from nine in the evening until nine the next morning. During the day he was not allowed to lie down or to sleep. The questions were always the same: did he admit to being a Socialist Revolutionary? Time and again, Jakubėnas denied the charge, explaining that in 1944 it was impossible to belong to a party that had ceased to exist in the 1920s (though we know from Šimaitė's correspondence that she attended underground Socialist Revolutionary meetings while she was visiting the ghetto). The court set his trial for December 27, and his brother Alfonsas, a lawyer, began organizing his defense. The prosecution entered "For Little Bird" as evidence against him, and Petras Cvirka, writer and president of the Writers' Union, testified that the poem could only be understood as anti-Soviet, citing Jakubėnas's behavior at a union meeting:

K. Jakubėnas bellowed that "the deported brothers must be repatriated." It doesn't take a genius to figure out which "brothers" he was talking about. There can be no doubt that K. Jakubėnas has demanded through his poetry that those "brothers," who murdered farmers — our very own Soviet citizens — only yesterday, and who have now been apprehended by our security services, be repatriated. Of course, K. Jakubėnas wrote anti-Smetona[1] poems, and during the German occupation wrote poetry denouncing the occupiers. He did this bravely and deserves credit for his anti-German work. But his anti-Soviet activity and behavior have negated any such credit due. (A. Jakubėnas 26)

Little could be gained by those who testified on Jakubėnas's behalf. People had been deported or executed on flimsier charges, and with more laughable evidence than poetry. Fear spread through the country, and even Jakubėnas's closest friends refused to speak in his defense at trial. The only person willing to testify on the poet's behalf was a professor who provided this written statement to the court:

During the German occupation, from 1940 to 1944 without interruption, Citizen Ona Šimaitė worked at the Vilnius State University Library. As far as we know the Germans transported her to Germany in 1944. We do not know her subsequent fate. Prof. J. Baldžius. July 16 1946. (A. Jakubėnas 26)

The text supported Jakubėnas's assertion that the poem was about Šimaitė and not about the mass deportations to Siberia.

Despite his brother's best efforts, Jakubėnas was sentenced to five years of hard labor. Alfonsas filed an official protest, claiming that no wrongdoing had been established. Fearing his brother would be sent to the far north, Alfonsas collected his warm jacket and headed to the local jail. Kazys was no longer there, but was *en route* to the coal mines of Kazakhstan.

Most of what we know about Kazys Jakubėnas's trial, imprisonment, exile, and death come from accounts his brother published in newspapers during the Glasnost and Perestroika years. Alfonsas Jakubėnas reveals little about himself in these texts, but immediately striking is the man's patience and persistence. He managed to tread the thin line that separated a private act from a criminal one under the Soviet justice system. An example of the line in her article that reads the secret police file as biography, Cristina Vatulescu explains that both the Romanian writer

Steinhardt and the secret police seem to have shared the belief that the complex process of religious conversion that the writer underwent in prison was a personal matter and as such deserved no reprimand. However, sharing the contents of that memoir, even if only with the typist, constituted a crime. Writing thus trod a thin line between criminal and innocent behavior. As a personal memoir it could be tolerated; however, inasmuch as its existence opened the possibility of a reader, writing was condemned. (256)

For a surprising number of years, Alfonsas Jakubėnas succeeded in locating this line in his brother's case, and against all odds, to work within a system that was capricious, paranoid, and characterized by "feverish efforts to misinform and to concoct secrets, plots, sabotages, and criminals" (Andreevich 101 qtd. in Vatulescu 252).

Thanks to Alfonsas's efforts to obtain a pardon, Kazys spent only seven months working hard labor. Like in the Tsarist prison camps, the majority of those imprisoned with him were Ukrainian political prisoners, also convicted of anti-Soviet activity, and aging Georgian Social Democrats sent into forced labor after their 1924 uprising. Each time their sentences were up, the authorities convicted them for another decade. The Georgians protected Kazys, taking his place in the mines and leaving him to work on a roof that needed reshingling. They told him his soft poet's hands were better suited to handing off nails and tacks than for hewing rock.

Kazys recounted this story to Alfonsas one day while walking through Vilnius. They sat down on a bench in Lenin Square, directly opposite the Secret Police building, where Kazys had been interrogated. A man and his wife walked by. Neither gave the two men sitting in the square a second glance, though from the way that his brother stared into their backs, Alfonsas was surprised they hadn't felt it. In a low voice, Kazys told Alfonsas that the man disappearing down Stalin Prospect, walking with such confidence outside the building where people were beaten and tortured every day, was Saakijanas, his interrogator.

"During my time in jail and in forced labor camp," Kazys told Alfonsas in a quiet voice,

I understood that nothing had changed in the Soviet Union. Politics are exactly the same now as they were before the war. While I was hiding in Samogitia during the war, I truly believed that life under the Soviets would bring more freedom. I thought that the conquered lands would reap a positive cultural shift. . . . I wanted to take part in this new life with all my energy, but as you can see, it hasn't worked out that way. (A. Jakubėnas 26)

Despite his pardon, between 1947 to 1950 Kazys Jakubėnas published nothing under his own name. He managed to print a handful of translations of Russian poetry under pseudonyms,[2] but his own work was destined for the drawer. Unemployed and unemployable, Kazys had no choice but to live with his brother. And even for this, he needed special permission from local police who would arrest anyone unemployed in Vilnius. When he managed to find a job selling books at a table in the street, the employer later rescinded the offer, explaining it would be unseemly for a well-known author to be doing such menial work. Eventually, Jakubėnas found a clerical position.

The day before his 1946 arrest Jakubėnas, together with all other

Lithuanian writers, attended a meeting to be dressed down. Writers whom the regime sanctioned (Petras Cvirka among them) told those gathered that they were unproductive, lazy, and that they were not doing their part as artists to further social change. Those assembled formed a ragged, harassed, and hungry bunch, in many cases lacking even bare necessities. Most stood silently as the anointed lectured, spewing patent untruths about how well off they were. The sharp-tongued Jakubėnas was unable to restrain himself. He stood up to speak:

I wasn't going to talk, but since the executive committee president has scolded us for inactivity and unwillingness to work, I've decided to say a few words about the current creative atmosphere. There are reasons to believe that those in the highest positions of authority are unfamiliar with these conditions and that it would be useful for them to get acquainted with what's going on. It's been stated a few times that writers now have very good working conditions, so I'd like to comment on them. The conditions, frankly, are not as good as some here would have us believe. Take me as an example. All day I have to work in an office to earn my bread. I can't really complain, since I'm quite privileged in this regard, and others have an even harder situation. Still, I'm left only with evenings for my writing. I try to use my evenings well. I come home, eat dinner, clean up, and pick up my pen. But before I've managed to sort out my thoughts, I hear someone beating the door down. "NKVD. We're here to search." "Fine, go to it," I say. For an hour they dump everything out of drawers, shake and throw things around, but find nothing. Except my leftover dinner in the cupboard, so they take that with them. No matter, I think, it's of no importance. I tidy up the room and try to sit down with my pen once again. But an hour later, someone's hammering at the door again. "Who is it?" I ask. "Military police. We're here to search." Again, a sizeable group of armed men forces its way into the room, and proceeds to turn everything upside down. These men don't find anything, since the first group left nothing of interest behind. And what could they possibly find? Even if there was something to find, it would be hard to locate. Smetona's and Himmler's police forces already taught us how to protect ourselves from them. So the military police finds nothing, and since there isn't even any food left for them to swipe, they grab my last items of clothing. Once this second group of armed men has gone, it's no longer possible to think about writing.

How can you ask us to work under these conditions? Do you really have the right to ask us to produce? As long as these conditions exist in Lithuania, do not demand texts from your writers. (Kateiva)

Jakubėnas made it home safely that night, but the next night an armed group of men came to his house. They carried away with them two suitcases of manuscripts, and the poet followed. Months later he was on his way to the coal mines of Kazakhstan. A few years after that he was dead.

CHAPTER 14

Kazys's Death

JANUARY 1950. Alfonsas returns to the room he shares with his brother. It is late, around midnight but Kazys is nowhere to be found. There is a note from a friend who came by to see his brother at 9:00 p.m., so he has been gone since earlier that evening. Alfonsas waits until the early morning, pacing and drinking tea, but Kazys never reappears. It is a cold night, with the temperature falling to minus thirty Celsius. Alfonsas begins to worry, suspecting that the secret police have taken his brother. First thing on January 8, he goes to see a friend and colleague, a lawyer who works on so-called special files to ask him if he can find out where Kazys is being held.

Two days later, Alfonsas is summoned by police. After a long interrogation, the police chief finally tells Jakubėnas that his brother "is no longer among the living." He goes on to explain that Kazys was found on the morning of January 8, frozen, naked to the waist and barefooted. He was found at Number 4 Kapų (Cemetery) Street, on the outskirts of Vilnius. The chief then describes how one of the tenants of Number 4 brought an unresponsive Jakubėnas into his apartment, and how the poet had died on the apartment's kitchen floor. When asked why it took so long to inform Alfonsas of his brother's death, the captain replies that the circumstances are very unclear. No one knows why Kazys was in such a remote corner of Vilnius in the middle of the night, how he came to lose his clothes, and why he had no identification. After long discussions with military police, Alfonsas is finally allowed to claim his brother's remains for burial, and a funeral is planned for January 15.

At midnight on the night before the funeral there is a knock at the door. A secret police envoy has come to escort Alfonsas to the same building where Kazys had been so mercilessly interrogated before his trial. At reception he dials the number that the envoy has given him, and is allowed to enter. Six men await him when he arrives at the door of the office, among them General Leonov. There he is told that the funeral is to remain a modest, if not secret, affair: no one but family members should be informed and no invitations may be extended. There is to be no fanfare, no music, no procession to the burial site, and only the route designated by Leonov himself is to be taken to the cemetery.

"Your brother was well known," declares the General, "and rumors are spreading throughout the city about his death."

The funeral is carried out according to orders, with only family and close friends present. In the early afternoon a horse-drawn hearse traces out the route from the hospital morgue to the Rasų cemetery gates. Wreath bearers walked in front of the horses, the mourners follow, and all around them lurk secret police dressed in civilian clothes. At the graveside there are no speeches. Only silence and cold. The only sound to be heard is fistfuls of earth hitting the coffin as mourners say their final farewells.

Alfonsas finds the circumstances of his brother's death suspicious. For a decade now, keeping his brother out of prison has been almost a full-time job. He has worked the system from within to protect Kazys. He knows the constitution, and the bizarre bureaucracy that is the Soviet administration. He is a patient and curious man. Something terrible happened to his brother, and Alfonsas needs to find out what. He begins to investigate on his own.

Number 4 Kapų Street is a large wooden house like you find in the country, so far off the beaten track is this street. Its roof slants sharply and a wood shed stands off to the right. Snow blankets the front yard and dried scrub pokes up through a dirty and trodden frozen layer. Alfonsas wonders if this is where his brother fell.

Too afraid to venture to the site of his brother's death on his own, Alfonsas has asked his friend, Jokūbas Lapašinskas, also a lawyer, to come with him to make inquiries.

First, they visit the family living on the south side of the building. They are self-described Party members, recently arrived from Russia with the Soviet occupiers. Two men lie in bed, fully dressed, like soldiers ready to burst into battle at a moment's notice. They even wear shoes. When Alfonsas and Lapašinskas enter the room, the men cover their faces with their hats, and refuse to speak or even acknowledge the visitors' presence. Only the women answer questions. Reluctantly, they admit to having heard shouts for help on the cold January night, but paid no attention because they had guests. Dinner served with a side of death in the front yard. Speechless, Alfonsas moves on to the second apartment.

On the same side of the building live an elderly couple named Savickis. They too acknowledge having heard cries, and even feared that the voice belonged to their son, brought back for interrogation from Poland. After listening carefully they realized with relief that the voice was not his. With a smile Savickis adds that whatever was going on outside, it was clearly a political matter, and that it was always better to stay out of situations like that.

On the northern end of the building lives the driver Klymov, on whose kitchen floor Kazys died. Recent arrivals, like the others, they claim to have heard shouts for help, and when the driver opened the door, he saw that Kazys was not alone. Once he collapsed, his assailant ordered Klymov to take the barely conscious poet inside.

"If he was still conscious, why didn't you ask who was doing this to him?" asks Alfonsas.

"I did," answered Klymov with a shrug. "But your brother just cursed at me and stuck out his tongue before he blacked out."

Upstairs from Klymov, in the last apartment, Alfonsas finds an elderly couple from Smolensk. They report hearing shouts, then men brawling. Initially they started down the stairs to see what the commotion was about, but returned to their apartment in fear when the cries for help shifted from outdoors to inside the downstairs flat, growing weaker, until finally — silence. After gathering the courage to investigate, they crept down to find a man lying on Klymov's kitchen floor. He had blond hair, blue eyes, and hands too delicate to be those of a laborer.

Alfonsas visits the scene of his brother's death twice more. On the first return he meets two secret police agents, who ask if he is Kazys's brother. To his surprise they claim to have known the poet very well, and note the similarity between the two brothers' voices, which strikes Alfonsas as peculiar. If the secret police knew his brother well enough to compare their voices, he wonders, why were they unable to identify him for so long?

By his final visit to Number 4 Kapų, the driver, Klymov, has disappeared, apparently repatriated to Russia. Suddenly it all comes together, and a revelation hits him: far from a good Samaritan, or even a driver, for that matter, Klymov had been among Kazys's tormentors. He took the poet into his kitchen not to revive him, but to watch him die. The secret police had hired Klymov to do away with Kazys.

Winter in Vilnius is long and gray, but spring brings little relief for Alfonsas, who is no closer to finding justice or solving his brother's death. The room they had shared, so cramped for the two of them, now feels empty and cavernous without the poet's beating heart. Alfonsas continues to see friends and to read, often taking Kazys's books off the shelf to caress, as if they contained a little of the man who once owned them. It is while sorting through his brother's books one day that he comes across a crucial piece of evidence: a savings account manual that Kazys had been translating on the evening he disappeared to earn a bit of cash. In the corner of his draft of the translation he had scribbled a telephone number: 2-31-67. When Alfonsas phones Information to inquire whose number this is, he learns that the number is restricted.

Strangely energized by the secrecy he encounters at every turn, Alfonsas writes and hand-delivers a letter to the Chairman of the Central Committee of Lithuania, A. Sniečkus. In it he outlines the suspicious circumstances of Kazys's death, Klymov's disappearance, and the unsatisfactory progress of the investigation. He appends a copy of the page of the draft with the secret phone number, and asks that it be identified, along with the names of any employees working in the corresponding office on the evening of Kazys's disappearance. The letter touches a nerve.

Three days later, there is a midnight knock at his door. Alfonsas walks slowly to the door, in no hurry to open it: only secret police come calling at this hour. The visitor tells him he must come to the Ministry of Internal Affairs immediately. Alfonsas has no choice. He dresses and heads out into the night with the stranger.

They are waiting for him when he arrives at the Ministry. Before he has a chance to sit down, the agent shouts at him from across his desk.

"How dare you suggest that the Ministry is involved in your brother's death?" he thunders.

Unprepared for the attack, Alfonsas steps back before speaking. "I've done no such thing."

The agent reaches into his desk and pulls out a thin file. Alfonsas recognizes his letter to the Central Committee Chairman together with Kazys's manuscript with phone number scrawled on the upper corner.

"What's this, if not an accusation?" The agent's voice is terse, but calmer.

Alfonsas answers that there is no accusation in the letter, only a query about a phone number. The agent says nothing, but moves the file pointedly, revealing a list of telephone numbers displayed under the glass desktop. Among the numbers, Alfonsas finds 2-31-67, the number from the manuscript. It corresponds to the very office they are sitting in.

As if to move on from the unpleasant revelation, the agent proceeds to offer a theory on Kazys's murder.

"Perhaps your brother had a lover outside the city whose husband beat him up and left him to freeze to death."

Alfonsas rejects this out of hand, trying to keep his voice steady as he answers that there was no such husband.

"Then maybe he was killed by nationalists. We found a bunker of theirs close to where he was killed."

Alfonsas again restrains himself and he shakes his head.

"Did you or did you not call my brother in for interrogation on the night of January 7?"

"Maybe we called him in, but that doesn't mean anything. Robbers could've attacked him after we sent him home and then taken him to Kapų Street to mug him there." He pauses before continuing. "Comrade Jakubėnas, I feel I need to tell you that your presence has twice been noted at the crime scene. If you want to keep your head, you'll stay out of this investigation. Our people will do the work to find out what happened."

"And why should I stay out of it?"

"Because the area around Kapų Street is a very dangerous place. We keep finding corpses there."

CHAPTER 15

Alfonsas's Theory

HERE is what Alfonsas believes happened.

On the evening of January 7, 1950, Kazys was in mid-translation of the bank pamphlet when an agent arrived to bring him to the Ministry. He gave Kazys a phone number to call for a building pass. Kazys noted the number on the translation, perhaps hoping to communicate to Alfonsas where he had gone. By the time Alfonsas returned home Kazys had most likely already been taken out to an interrogation center near Number 4 Kapų Street.

Despite promises to do so, no findings from the investigation into Kazys's death were ever made public. No one was ever brought to justice, though in 1954 the military high court condemned to death a secret police minister and a major-general for fabricating cases against party officials. Together with them, the court convicted General Leonov, who Alfonsas believed orchestrated Kazys's murder. In 1956 Kazys was posthumously pardoned, and writers who had originally testified against him at trial now called publicly for the republication of the slain poet's work. Small consolation to Alfonsas or to his brother, buried in Rasų Cemetery without so much as a eulogy.

Šimaitė never recovered from Jakubėnas's death. In her correspondence to Alfonsas, Šimaitė repeated her promise to write a short memoir about him. Among her papers at Vilnius University is a file containing clippings, notes and a short manuscript about her friend, the beginnings of the promised memoir. The text never saw the light of day, and Šimaitė probably considered it unfinished.

Her 1964 letter to a young novelist hints at the depth of the wound that prevented her from writing about the poet:

And when you mentioned Kazys Jakubėnas, you gave me a real scare. I know a lot, but I can't write, or something else happens. I don't know why this is so. And now I just get scared. Would it not be better to put an end to it all and just put up a large cross? Nowadays even letter writing is too much for me. (Letter to Icchokas Meras, January 31, 1964, Meras's Papers)

There is a scene in Milan Kundera's, *The Book of Laughter and Forgetting,* where the only evidence of a man's presence (after he is erased from a photograph) is his hat that sits on another man's head. I've often thought of Jakubėnas's story as a chalk outline left behind at a crime scene after the police have gone home. A life was lived, a dramatic death suffered, but all we really have of this story is the outline left behind. The substance of life has been erased, and with the first rainstorm or floor washing, the last evidence of it will disappear.

After the Soviet erasure of Jakubėnas, what has remained? A few poems for children, a handful of books for adults, an article his brother wrote, and an unfinished memoir by Ona Šimaitė, his friend.

PART FIVE

CHAPTER 16

Catholicism, Sex, and Sin

ŠIMAITĖ'S worldview consisted of a curious blend of anarchism and Catholicism. While her diaries record that she had little patience for government and bureaucracy, for an anarchist, she carried a lot of self-doubt, self-judgment, and even self-hatred. In this respect she was a good Catholic. Either repressed or simply asexual in temperament, Šimaitė was silent in both her letters and diaries on the subjects of sex and physical pleasures other than good food or a nice bath. The polar opposite of anarchist Emma Goldman, who embraced sex and shunned conventional marriage, Šimaitė's comments on the subject underscore her birth into a conservative Catholic tradition and its vocabulary of sin and morality:

I read Françoise Sagan's Dans un mois, dans un an *(In a month, in a year). . . . It's about physical love. Without any spiritual experience they get together and split up, and then start all over again. Just as in her first two books, here too she depicts youth as devoid of any morality, without any ideas. Bourgeois youth. But, to be fair, it must be said that even the greatest idealist and moralist searching for eternal and singular love — does he not give in easily to the body's desires? Everyone has so much weakness and sin. This is why we can't throw stones at Sagan. Who among us is without sin?* (January 27, 1958, Diary 19)

She determined her fate in so far as her private life was concerned: there is no evidence of a sexual life, and her pronouncement on

women's biological fate is unequivocal — in her 1956 diary she calls
menstruation, childbirth, and menopause "an endless tragedy, a
catastrophe, and a barbarity of nature" (April 21, 1956, Diary 11).
Is it possible that while trying to escape a perceived biological
determinacy (marriage, motherhood, dependence on men), Šimaitė
nevertheless got caught in another trap? Had her body become such
a burden that it seemed easier to shed bones, skin, and muscle and
move on as a disembodied spirit?

The absence of a sexual life or even sexual identity in Šimaitė's
papers has long puzzled me. If she had a lover, she does not say so,
and if she desires a sex life, there is no indication. The only concrete
evidence of love in Šimaitė's life is a Spanish love poem written to
her in July 1946 at a spa in the Beaujolais region of France, where she
convalesced with survivors and members of the resistance. "Ona,"
the Lithuanian version of "Anne," here becomes "Ana":

> *To separate myself from you, dear Ana*
> *Is the same as to rob me of my existence*
> *Which is my heart and my consciousness*
>
> *My soul will be saddened without you*
> *And my life in continuous pain.*
> *I lament the sad departure*
> *That I see coming with vehemence.*
> (*Šimaitė's, Papers, F244–357, Vilnius University*)

The signature "Antonio" and photograph of a middle-aged man
with dark hair and sharp cheek bones accompany the poem. Who
was he? Was the love mutual? Consummated? I have no idea. This
short text is the only trace of him.

But when I find it in the Vilnius University archives, I am happy
to know that Šimaitė was loved. And that she'd experienced the
sweetness of what it is to be adored.

I've come to believe that (certainly after the war, and perhaps
leading up to it as well) Šimaitė lived a celibate life, like a secular

monk or nun, devoted to a contemplative life, to poverty, and to service to others. In earlier times, she would have made a good saint. By the time she arrived in France her body bore scars of torture, and she had come very close to martyrdom — death for her beliefs. For Šimaitė, her body seems to have been little more than a vessel for her mind.

Recently I turned on the television to find a special about Shakers, and only had to watch for a few minutes before I became engrossed. Several things have stuck with me: the stunning simplicity of the work of the Shaker craftspeople, their incredible self-sufficiency, and that their historical leaders were women. But what struck me most of all was the idea of work as worship: a notion that makes absolute sense to me, and I think would have made sense to Šimaitė as well. In her journals she regularly referred to museums and art galleries as her churches, and to her early morning mending (during the war years, when she was visiting the ghetto) as prayer. But even more markedly, for Šimaitė, reading and writing were forms of worship. She rose early in the morning and worked all day before falling into bed at night with a book. Add this to the fact that celibacy was a way of life for her, and one has a very good candidate for the Shaker life indeed.

But for all her Shaker-like service to others, Šimaitė's diaries reveal a deeply held belief that she herself was unworthy of love or kindness, to the extent that she interpreted acts of generosity toward her as a form of punishment. In 1958, a care package from her brother in Vilnius brought her little pleasure, since she could only see it as confirmation of her unworthiness and a reminder of a regretted wartime incident, when she judged and punished her brother for not upholding his end of a bargain. No matter that the incident had likely prolonged and even saved lives in the ghetto, or that her actions had long since been forgiven and forgotten, to Šimaitė, her sin toward her brother remained unredeemed and unredeemable:

Such a generous gift from my brother's family feels as if it's a punishment. I never understood him, scolded him very harshly, and accused him of being incapable of keeping his word. And once I behaved cruelly and unjustly with him. I once gave him a good blanket. He paid for half of it with the bread and lard that the Jews in the ghetto needed so badly. And when he didn't pay the second half of his debt on time, I went and took back the blanket while he wasn't home and sold it to a speculator for half price . . .¹ Many years have passed, and I can't forget this. I burn with shame, and guilt eats away at me. Sometimes you can be punished through the kindness of others. And I've earned this punishment! How small I am in comparison to him. And even now some people continue to call me "good." But this is my bloody secret that nobody knows. My guilty conscience. What a terrible punishment. (Diary 19)

Where did this deep sense of unworthiness come from?

Šimaitė had been a faithful Catholic into young adulthood. She had loved the rituals and language of the Church. The Latin murmurings of the long-robed priest, and the humility of receiving communion on her knees. She used to savor the red patches and creases on her legs as scars of her faith and proof of her fervor. The incense made her head swoon, and on some Sundays Šimaitė reached a state of near-ecstasy, inventing the story of her own martyrdom and sainthood, a narrative cobbled together from the stories she had received throughout childhood: Saint Sebastian, crucified, and Joan of Arc, burned at the stake.

But faith left her when she left Lithuania for Moscow. Suddenly, in the enormous city, with its galleries, theaters, and revolution in the air, the roadside chapels and the wooden statuettes of Christ in rural Lithuania seemed primitive and rough. Her student years were ones of financial impoverishment, but of cultural riches: Šimaitė visited the Tretyakov Gallery regularly, and went to see Isadora Duncan dance at every opportunity. At night in her tiny room, she would read Russian poetry by Baltrušaitis and Esenin.

In the winter of 1917 Šimaitė's mother, father, and three siblings also found themselves in Russia. They had moved east to Tsaritsyn with a Riga factory that produced train compartments. The war was on, and production needed to continue, but in a safer place. On Christmas Eve of that year, the family heard a knock on the door. Outside a wicked blizzard was howling, and they wondered if a stranger had arrived seeking shelter. But when they opened the door, they found Šimaitė standing on the threshold. With tears in their eyes, her brother and sister threw their arms around her.

The table was laden with traditional foods: herring, black bread, beet salad. The family members sat down to their feast, but first were invited to make the sign of the cross, to give thanks for the food, and to ask for blessings in the coming year. Šimaitė refused. Her mother insisted. Šimaitė refused again. In the end, Šimaitė took her coat and went back out into the blizzard, heeding her mother's command to "go back to where she came from" if she didn't have the decency to respect tradition. Šimaitė's father's efforts to calm the atmosphere failed. It was the last time the entire family ever gathered (Šimas 11). The following year, 1919, Šimaitė's father died of typhus. Shortly after, in 1919, her mother followed. Both lie buried in the Tsaritsyn cemetery. Their children were left to fend for themselves.

The break with her family was something that Šimaitė came bitterly to regret. Years later she wrote in a letter:

Over the past few days I've seen her in my dreams, and even while awake, I've spent entire days crying for my mother. . . . I was far away when she died. How I would like to know what her final hours were like, and where and how she was buried. You can't know how much I miss her now. Like never before.

How short a person's life is. And sometimes we unwillingly hurt the ones we love most. (Šimaitė qtd. in Šimas 11)

Šimaitė's niece, Aldona Šakalinytė, in Kaunas, agreed to do some detective work for her and sent back an account of Šimaitė's mother's death:

MARCH 10, 1958

My dear Aunt,

I asked my mother to tell me about her mother's death. She was very reluctant to talk about it, and only gave me bits and pieces of the story. She said she didn't want to cause you pain. So, what I'm about to write is a composite of what she's now told me and of what I know from before.

After grandfather's death, grandmother got sick with cancer. . . . The city fell into the hands of the White Guard, and then changed hands several times more. There was famine. There was no bread, so what hope was there to get medicine? You can imagine the pain she had to suffer. She was ill for six months. . . . Before she died, she kissed my mother's hands and asked her to take care of the children, especially Kaziukas [her youngest son]. She loved him a great deal. She wanted him to go into the priesthood. She asked to be buried next to her husband. Death was a salvation for her, but for everyone else, it presented a new worry: getting a coffin. And, according to my mother, that's when a miracle happened. A strange woman approached my mother when she was sitting at the edge of a ditch crying, overcome by hopelessness. Judging from her appearance and accent, she was neither Russian nor Ukrainian. She was from the East. After listening to my mother's story, she told her she had two sons and three coffins, one for each family member. She offered my mother one of the coffins. Mother was overjoyed. A few days went by and the corpse had begun to smell, but there was still no way to transport it to the cemetery seven kilometers away. Mama told me that they felt very anxious and afraid. All the other refugees had left and she was left alone in this strange place with the children. Except there was a woman from Riga . . . who helped Mother here. That woman and a friend were searching the whole city for any vehicle, even a bicycle, when they bumped into an acquaintance who was flirting with a White Guard soldier. She managed to get him to lend her a wonderful carriage and horse for grandmother's funeral. She had lied and told him that the carriage was for a wedding, otherwise (without the prospect of a big party), he never would have given it. And so they decorated her coffin with acacia blossoms, took grandmother to the cemetery and buried her in the same grave where grandfather had been buried earlier. All the mourners who traveled with her risked a bullet to the forehead, because there was unrest in the city.

(Aldona Šakalinytė, Šimaitė's Papers, Vilnius University)

After burying their mother, Liuda, Julija and Kaziukas took a circuitous route back to Lithuania, sailing across the Black Sea. They finally landed in a shelter in Vilnius. One cold night, as we wandered the old town's dark streets, Šimaitė's nephew Kęstutis, Kaziukas's son, and I happened upon it. Now a youth hostel, I suppose it still sees its share of weary travelers.

16. Sala Vaksman/Tanya Shterntal with her husband in a German displaced persons camp after the war. Vilnius University Library Rare Books and Manuscripts Department.

CHAPTER 17

Mothering

WITH no husband or discernable lover in her life, it should come as no surprise that Šimaitė was never a biological mother. What may be surprising is how she nonetheless mothered in her life.

Although celibate, Šimaitė conceived of a child, a navel-less child.[1] She unofficially adopted Sala, the young university student she rescued from the ghetto and hid in the library. Though Sala was in her twenties when the two women met, both considered the relationship to be that of a parent and child. Their bond grew stronger after the war. Šimaitė's earliest reference to Sala as her daughter occurs in a 1950 letter to Marc Dworzhetsky (Dworzhetsky's Papers, Yad Vashem).

Postwar Germany and Israel were places of extraordinary self-reinvention, and Sala Vaksman is a good illustration. Already she had two names. In addition to her given name, Sala had a pen name, Ktana, that Šimaitė often used in reference to her. After the war, Sala took a third name, and became Tanya, which is what she called herself until the end of her life. Šimaitė explained this final name change in a letter to Dworzhetsky: "In the [DP] camp there was a woman who looked after [Ktana]. She had lost a daughter named Tanya. This woman asked Ktana to call herself Tanya. That's where her new name came from" (Dworzhetsky's Papers, April 13, 1950, Yad Vashem). Perhaps in taking on another daughter's name,

Sala/Ktana/Tanya was ready to reinvent herself further. She was ready to take on a new mother, whom she found in Šimaitė. If her first mother had conceived her, Šimaitė, this second mother, had sustained her.

In 2002 I traveled from Jerusalem to Tel Aviv to meet Tanya's son, Shlomo, and her granddaughter, Merav. Shlomo had been only four years old when he first met his adoptive grandmother and was living at Kibbutz Reshafim in the north of Israel when Šimaitė arrived early in 1953. Shlomo remembers tickling the soles of her feet, saying she liked how his small fingers felt on the scars left by her Vilnius interrogators. Life on the kibbutz was hard, too hard and too hot for Šimaitė. Although she loved the communal way of life and the idea of living off the land, lacking the strength to earn her keep, she could not live there.

Eventually, after three months at Kibbutz Reshafim, she was allocated a small apartment in Petach Tikva, a town between Jerusalem and Tel Aviv. She didn't visit Tanya often, since the journey was long, and she suffered from the pressure of unanswered letters, unfinished translations, and never-ending housework. On March 7, 1954, she wrote in her diary of a recent trip north to visit Tanya and her family:

I was very tired yesterday and had heart palpitations during the night. I had wanted to get up at 4:00, but ended up sleeping in until 6:00. I regret the time wasted sleeping. I prepared for the journey and wrote two letters. We left at noon, and by 5:00 we were at the kibbutz.

The kibbutz is a village with well-tended fields. The people at the kibbutz are so kind and simple. Even though the kibbutz is very poor, they take care of their sick and of their children. They even designated a separate bathhouse and toilet for me, this old woman. It was very moving. They've made great progress in one year. After five years of endless work, the people there are very tired. Even the rabbi's daughter was complaining of fatigue. They live right on the border, that is, right at the wolf's jaws.

The journey to see Tanya ate up a great deal of time, not to mention my constant need for rest. Time is such a resource, and it never returns. And my debt repayment is at a standstill. I had no right to go, but those who love me cannot understand this. At home, it would have been otherwise, and I wouldn't have been knocked off my feet in the same way. But you have to give what is human over to humanity. And I have to continue to shoulder my burden.

The biggest pleasure was bathing every day, sharing in the beauty of nature, and the human kindness of the kibbutz. We spent two days sewing Shlomo's prince costume — the whole kibbutz was getting ready for Purim.

On March 15 I returned to Petach Tikva. (Diary 4)

But first impressions can be misleading.

Though Šimaitė marveled at the utopian life on the kibbutz upon her arrival, calling the children's houses "real little palaces," later in her journals she wrote of how Shlomo missed his mother, and wanted to live with her "like they do in the city. To go to school, and eat lunch together afterward" (July 23, 1956, Diary 13). Driving me back to the bus station after our interview, Shlomo began spontaneously to tell me how unhappy he had been as a child. The communal children's houses where he had grown up, he said matter-of-factly, were a cruel way to raise children.

The idea had been, he explained, to share everything, even children. It didn't work. Kibbutzim now have stopped the practice, but those separated from their parents as children, continue to file lawsuits.

Today Shlomo is a painter, and Merav, a teacher who translates for her father, is nine months pregnant with Šimaitė's adoptive great-great-grandson. She gave birth a few days after our meeting. I recorded our conversation on an old tape recorder borrowed from Yad Vashem, assuring a shy and nervous Shlomo that I had no plans to make a radio documentary. We began by comparing notes on the story of how Šimaitė took Tanya out of the ghetto. In the archives at Yad Vashem, I had read that Šimaitė led Tanya out under a coat, but Shlomo corrected me, saying "in a bag of potatoes."[2] He and Merav added simultaneously that yes, indeed,

Tanya had been very small and very thin. "And Anya," as Tanya and her family called Šimaitė, "was very strong."

When I raised the question of the mother-daughter relationship between the two, Merav confirmed that the feeling had been mutual. Tanya too considered Šimaitė to be her mother, "because her mother left when she was quite young. . . . Her parents separated." The separation had been a source of intense shame for Tanya, and she'd rarely talked about it. Merav and her siblings "learned of all these things much later." Like so many other survivors, Tanya seems to have wanted to shake off her past and start anew in Israel: new name, new mother, new life. Shame at the abandonment by her mother kept Tanya from giving testimony to Yad Vashem about Šimaitė for many years.

Merav and Shlomo do not know their (great-) grandmother's name, but they told me as much as they could about the mystery surrounding her death. From Poland, Tanya's mother made her way to France where she had a child by her second husband, a member of the French resistance during the war. When they found themselves in the Occupied Zone, she gave her husband money to pay someone to take her over the border. She never made it and likely died in the camps. Merav and Shlomo suspect that her husband turned her in.

When Tanya traveled to Paris in 1959, Šimaitė tracked down the second husband so that he could share details of how his wife, Tanya's mother, had died. When he refused, Šimaitė calmly threatened to go to the authorities with everything she knew about his conduct during the war. "He didn't know what she knew," explained Merav, "so the husband was finally convinced, and he came to meet Tanya when she was in France. It was a very unpleasant meeting. He thought she was looking for money, but she said she only wanted to know what happened to her mother. He didn't really give any details."

How should we understand this gesture of adopting an adult daughter, or accepting a new mother in the prime of life? Is this mothering of the mind, rather than of the body? Was Šimaitė's mothering the result of ghettos and hiding places? Were her birthing pains deportation, interrogation, and hunger? But perhaps she was mothering long before she met Tanya and made it official. Through her support of POWs, her clandestine visits to the ghetto, her attempts to disentangle questions of individual and collective blame after the war, and even in her decision to accept compensation from the Germans (in a gesture of reconciliation), Šimaitė was also mothering. Her mothering preceded motherhood.

And as for the land of Šimaitė's dreams? She returned to Paris three years after arriving in Israel, desperately unhappy, and longing for the French capital's cultural treasures. One souvenir she brought home went undetected for years. Only in 1959, after several hospitalizations and years of battling pain, fever, and dizziness did she learn that the culprit was malaria, courtesy of Kibbutz Reshafim.

PART SIX

CHAPTER 18

Ludelange

JULY 2007

Ludelange appears on no map, and when we arrive there, it becomes clear why. It's tiny. The village is one of three that made up the *commune* of Tressange. The woman at our hotel's front desk marks it on a map for us, but only after we've found its location for her by internet. Even the locals don't know where it is, and it's only twenty minutes away.

At the roundabout in Tressange we take a guess and turn right toward the *mairie* to see if we can find someone to talk to. There's a wedding on, and the central square is packed with cars. The region has seen better days. By the church we find a monument to the *commune*'s iron miners, and at the bean-shaped roundabout stand a mining car and crane, vestiges of the former economic heart of this community.

After parking on what looks to be someone's front stoop, I follow the signs to the library, but get distracted by the open door at the Centre socio-culturel. I don't make it three steps in the door before a man with glasses jumps out at me, kisses me on both cheeks, and inquires what he can do to help *cette fille*. When I explain that we're looking for Ludelange and why, he informs me that we're in the village of Tressange. At the roundabout we should have turned left instead of right. As for the history of the internment camp, he suggests that we talk to ninety-two-year-old Monsieur Jammes.

The suggestion is seconded by the jogger he stops to consult. The mayor might know something, they add, but he's busy singing in the wedding choir.

Sean, baby Sebastian, and I make our way to Monsieur Jammes's house across the street from the village square. He initially looks alarmed to find three strangers there (although one of us is admittedly very small), but invites us in for an Orangina after we introduce ourselves. He tells us that he knows that there was a camp here, where Germans held Russian POWs. The military barracks, the site of the camp, were destroyed some fifteen years ago. Only the gates remain. Two posts flank what was once its entrance. Now only a pile of rubble lies where soldiers, Šimaitė, and other prisoners once lived.

Monsieur Jammes is happy to tell us what he can about the military camp, but this is not much. For most of the war he was a prisoner in Germany, just north of Berlin, and can think of no one else in the village of his age who might have been here during the war.

After two days we have to leave. We haven't learned much about the camp, but we've seen the landscape Šimaitė would have seen, with its rolling hills and grazing cows, its expansive fields, and the vestiges of once-busy mines that are now quiet. Thionville, the city closest to Ludelange, is an ugly industrial town made up mostly of prefab planned communities. Our hotel there, like Tressange, has seen better days. Its carpets are shabby and towels threadbare, and the dining room has a spectacular view of the decidedly unspectacular town. But the food is fantastic, and everyone we come across is helpful and friendly. I assume that Šimaitė probably had little opportunity to enjoy the warm character of the locals. Under German guard, and convalescing from injuries acquired from her interrogations by the Gestapo, Šimaitė likely spent little time outside the prison camp. So, I am startled when, many months later, I come across a mention of Thionville in a Paris diary. Even there, in that ugly little city, and after months of suffering, Šimaitė managed to scope out a corner of beauty and culture. "I still remember

Thionville and the unforgettable painting I saw there," she wrote on Christmas Day of 1957. "Christ was high on a hill, dying on the cross by himself. All around him is terrifying darkness. Around the base of the cross coils a triumphant snake" (Diary 19). The painting she describes depicts the darkest moment before the resurrection. Perhaps she found solace in this painting, and could believe that she too would come through her ordeal and find new life at the end of the war.

When Americans liberated Ludelange in September 1944, Šimaitė began her trip southward to the Soviet internment camp at La Courtine in the Limousin region of France. Four months later she left La Courtine for Toulouse.

CHAPTER 19

Freedom

IN 1945 the Allies began implementing a short-lived policy of forcibly returning Soviet citizens. Since Lithuania was now under Soviet occupation, Šimaitė found herself in danger of being deported to the USSR. The possibility frightened her. She believed she would likely be deported to Siberia after returning to Lithuania, because of her prewar political activity and sympathies for the Socialist Revolutionaries; and she also feared it would be impossible to contact family members and friends of the ghetto dead in the West from inside the Soviet Union. With the help of a friend, Šimaitė managed to convince French authorities to surrender her to the Polish government in exile, rather than to the Soviets as planned, which allowed her to remain in France. She describes the episode in a letter to Isaac Nachman Steinberg. A negative reproduction of the Russian manuscript, turning Šimaitė's script to white on a background black as night, is archived among Steinberg's papers in New York. As in all her letters to him, here she refers to her addressee in the third person:

Since I hid documents or knew about their hiding places, I considered it my responsibility to inform Jewish organizations about them. I couldn't remember a single overseas address, but I knew that I needed to do this before returning to Lithuania. Lithuania was already occupied by the Soviets at that time. Under any other regime it wouldn't have been difficult to [communicate with Jewish organizations and relatives]. But under the Bolsheviks, a person finds oneself completely dependent on the State. Of course, it would have been impossible to write anything to Steinberg at all.

At first it didn't even enter my head to stay in France, even though I very much wanted to travel around France, once fate had brought me here.

After liberation, the camps were taken over by the French. The head of our camp was a very kind young woman [who] behaved very compassionately toward me, and encouraged me to write a letter that she would send through the French Red Cross. I wrote a letter saying that I would like to speak or meet with someone responsible for representing the Jewish people, and then wrote a second letter to Mikhail Shur with the news that Grigory Shur had left him a chronicle and a few documents from the Vilna Ghetto. (Steinberg's Papers, no date [1946])

Grigory Shur had recorded his impressions of the ghetto and its events in thirty-nine hidden notebooks. He entrusted these to Šimaitė who stashed them in a metal box under two floorboards in the university library's attic. He died in Stutthof (Šuras 167). The documents were found after the war when Šimaitė wrote a letter to the Jewish Museum that was established in Vilnius in 1944, indicating its hiding place. The museum was short-lived and was closed promptly as a result of Stalin's anti-Semitic policies. Shur's notes then made their way to the Museum of Revolutionary History, where a friend of Shur's daughter worked and clandestinely copied the manuscript using a typewriter. When Shur's daughter Miriam left the USSR in 1960, she took the copy with her (Šuras, Intro 18). It was published in Lithuanian in 1997.

Šimaitė's letter to Steinberg continues:

After all the misery of the Poles, Italians, Spaniards, and Bulgarians, the Americans finally took us away from the camp at Ludelange. All Russian and Baltic civilians were handed over to the Soviet command in France. . . . On December 14, 1944, we were . . .[1] brought to the South of France, to the Soviet camp La Courtine . . . , where we were supposed to wait . . .[2]

At the camp run by the French ministry for detainees and deportees there was a French officer who spoke Russian. I once talked to him about what was going on. He told me that in Limoges there was a Ministry for Jewish

Affairs. He advised me to write a letter, which he offered to deliver . . .[3]
*On December 25, 1944, I delivered the letter to him. Three weeks passed
without a reply.*

*In the [next] camp of 5,000 people, there was a small group of Poles who
didn't want to be in the Soviet camp. One beautiful January day, a French
officer appeared at the camp and promised the Poles that in 7–8 days they
would be transferred out. He even asked one of my Polish friends how the
Jews in the camp were being treated. There were a few in our camp, but they
continued to conceal their Jewish identities, even from the Soviet authorities.
. . . The French officer wanted me to come see him. I arrived. He addressed
me in Polish "You're from Wilno? Would you like to be free?" I was speechless — freedom! I answered "yes," but added that before doing anything, I
needed to speak to him. . . .*

*8 days later Polish officers appeared. I went to the office. There I listened
to how they negotiated for every single person in the camp. I had little hope
that I would make it out of the Soviet camp. But then I decided to finish
with camp life. If they didn't give me my freedom, I would escape from the
Soviet camp. My Polish friend also whispered to me, "Say that your parents
were born and lived in Warsaw." This wouldn't matter much, since I had
been arrested in Vilnius, and Vilnius now belonged to the Soviets, as did I.
I . . . started to argue heatedly with the Soviet representatives. In the end,
after much debate, I succeeded by causing a great commotion, and was
officially handed over together with those people being returned to the Polish
provisional government in London! (Steinberg's Papers, no date [1946])*

The Allies shuffled Šimaitė from camp to camp ever southward until
they finally set her free in the southwestern city of Toulouse. Built
of pink, maroon, and red brick, "la ville rose" is historically one
of France's poorest cities, isolated for centuries by the mountains
to its north. But here too, things were changing. The language of
the region, Occitan, was dying, replaced by a twangy and lilting
French, in which every letter is pronounced, including the silent
es. For a foreigner like Šimaitė, this slow and careful speech is often
easier to understand than the northern accent, where half-words
are inhaled like cigarette smoke.

When she was not working, Šimaitė walked. Traditional *oustals
toulisaines,* urban dwellings with brick façades and wooden shut-

ters, lined the narrow and winding streets of the city. As in Vilnius, medieval church spires punctuated Toulouse's panorama. The sight of men smoking while they played *pétanques* in the parks comforted her. It was good to see signs of normality returning to this bruised and battered city. Even months after it ended, war continued to dominate life. It would be almost a year before cinemas reopened and commercial life on the streets resembled what it once had been. For now, a black market flourished, inflation continued to rise, and shortage was everywhere. Less than half the city's population was working, and even the employed had trouble making ends meet, so Šimaitė felt fortunate for her job at a cafeteria, hard as it was.

Toulouse gained 50,000 residents over the course of the war, bringing the total population to 260,000, and it was having trouble absorbing them all. Housing was scarce, and finding a decent apartment difficult. Overcrowding existed all over postwar France, but Toulouse had the distinction of offering some of the worst housing in the country.

The city's troubles transformed it at night. Bandits and armed former resistance fighters, reduced to pillaging, stealing ration cards, trafficking in black market foods and illegal weapons, now roamed the streets. The police patrolled nocturnally, checking identity papers. Because of all of this, Šimaitė rarely went out after dark, but spent her evenings writing letters.

17. Toulouse. Photo by the author.

CHAPTER 20

Toulouse

SEAN tells me that Roman cities like Toulouse are often red. The Romans produced bricks on site, then built with them. "Think of Bath," he says. "Those red brick ruins in the lush hills of southwest England." But beyond Toulouse the land is green and gold. The sunflowers have finished their blooms, and stand in the fields with heads hung. It's been a long two months getting here. Sean has been working in archives with papyri while I've occupied myself with the baby and try to stay cheerful despite the cold and rainy summer of monumental floods. We got out of Oxford a day before water submerged the county, and Berlin wasn't much better. But Toulouse welcomes us with its sun and golden landscapes, and now it's my turn to work.

We like Toulouse immediately. From the bridges you can look down on neighborhoods and see how the city has been pieced together like a jigsaw puzzle. All the red-tiled roofs are interconnected. It's a wonderful chaotic jumble. Sean remarks how peaceful it is along the Garonne, the river that winds through the city. Perhaps it is the city's traditional poverty that has kept it so. Underdeveloped, the river bank is for the people of the city, rather than for tourists or merchants. Spanning its waters is the Pont Neuf, the river's oldest bridge constructed in a series of arches. Beside the bridge stand the École des beaux arts and a seafood restaurant, on whose terrace a young man wearing a chain-mail glove shucks oysters.

Eventually we make it to Number 1 rue Théodore Ozenne. It is the only address I have associated with Šimaitė in this city. She didn't live in the building, but received her mail at this address, care of the ujj, L'Union de la jeunesse juive (The Union of Jewish Youth), founded in 1943 by Jewish communists. Now there is a fine foods shop occupying the main floor. Number 1 rue Ozenne is narrow, with two lacy iron balconies and a half-story that houses servants' quarters; it is the only kind of accommodation that people like Šimaitė could afford. The building itself is the last sliver in a long wall of edifices before the wall begins to curve around a shallow corner. The highest apartments around the vast intersection boast rooftop terraces and the trees that line the streets look to be about twenty years old. The neighborhood seems wealthy, though this was certainly not always the case.

Toulouse's churches, on the other hand, are wonderfully shabby. The cathedral is a vast and asymmetrical structure erected on the site of a Roman-era Christian church. Part of it is built in white stone, and the rest of it — most of it — is built in the red Toulouse brick. Inside we find more signs of the city's poverty. The frescoes and paintings that cover the cathedral's walls are now peeling. In some areas time has worn through paint and plaster, right back to the bricks. It's beautiful. The wear and tear of this cathedral show how much it has been loved over the centuries, like a favorite book. As I make my way from chapel to chapel, I almost bump into a woman replacing flowers and who has the serene face of one who works in churches.

People still pray here. This time I light a candle for my late father and one for Šimaitė as well.

I imagine Šimaitė visited Toulouse's churches. Their black Madonnas and plaques and notes of thanks for miracles and answered prayers must have reminded her of Vilnius, its churches, and the shrine at the Gates of Dawn. She loved architecture, history, biblical stories, and figures. And despite her professed atheism, I think she had a kind of affection for the Catholicism of both her native and adopted countries. She preferred simplicity, so I think that she too would have liked these peeling interiors, with altars made of nothing more than naked slabs of wood.

In October of 1945 Šimaitė sits at a desk illuminated by candlelight writing letters destined for America, South Africa, and Israel to the friends and family of the Vilna dead. The letters tell the stories of how her friends lived in the ghetto: the cramped conditions, the disappearances, secret births, and the ever-present illness and death. She begins each letter by repeating a promise she made: that she would deliver news of them if she survived the war. Šimaitė lacks the words to comfort her addressee. Her own suffering overpowers her ability to find the appropriate phrases, and she says so in her letter. It is a rare moment of openness.

She is always exhausted after long workdays, but still she writes late into the night. Terrible dreams torment her regularly, so she prefers to put off sleep for as long as possible, and manages to survive on three or four hours of rest.

At fifty-one, Šimaitė feels old beyond her years. Pain, this "gift from the Gestapo," is now her constant companion and her ever-present fatigue only makes things worse. Her face is wide, with strong cheekbones and jaw, but now her brow is more deeply furrowed than ever before and a haunted look clouds her once bright blue eyes. The Germans cut her hair, but once it grows back she will again wear it in two braids wrapped over the crown of her head.

Here in Toulouse she has no money, little command of French, and no friends. But what matters now is the freedom that she savors on her way to the market after work, at the Sunday concerts in the city's churches, and when she closes her eyes to listen to the candle flicker in the nighttime silence. After the horror of the camps she desires only to live according to her own rhythms and schedule and to earn her way in the world. Even the hardest work and longest hours can't dampen the pleasure and relief at once again having her own room. In her first weeks of freedom, she worked in Toulouse as a kitchen maid drying dishes for fourteen to seventeen hours per day. Now she toils ten to twelve hours a day in a cafeteria. All this makes it difficult for her to write at any other time than at night, yet the obligation to do so weighs on her increasingly. She spends her nonworking hours writing letters and fulfilling her promise to deliver the stories of the dead.

One of the first letters she writes in 1945 is on behalf of Anna Abramowicz and her daughter Dina. In her letter to Steinberg, Šimaitė devotes a few paragraphs to the women and to her attempts to aid them:

A few times I got to see Dina Abramowicz. She is the former librarian of the Jewish Children's library. She is in the city. She broke out of the ghetto and into the city because she was suffering there. And she wanted to get some food in the city. At 5:00 p.m. she returned to the ghetto tired, tortured . . . with two carrots.[1] Besides the enslavement, above all Dina suffers from having nowhere to undress and bathe like a human being.

Dina and her mother live together with their relatives, the Schreibers. In the one sunny room there are 9 people. One bed, two chairs, one table — the sum total of the furniture. All the other belongings and things are piled into a corner. The mountain reaches the ceiling. Along the windows are some dishes. The room is washed out twice a day. This room seems like a kind of oasis in the darkness of the ghetto. Professor Mowszowicz, who has arrived with me, can't rejoice enough that here in this room live cultured people, like-minded people, unlike at his own place, where a scientist is regarded as strangely as a white crow.

Here we can converse openly and speak our minds without constraint. There is a conversation about the day the Jews were sent to the ghetto. Painfully, I report to them that I saw almost no sympathy for the Jews. The engineer Schreiber tells how his family encountered small comforts, like the Lithuanian soldier who was to lead them in a convoy to the ghetto, and who behaved like a human being. He advised them not to hurry and to prepare carefully. He opened the cupboards himself and collected necessities for them. When everything was packed, he led them to the ghetto quietly and peacefully. Having finished his story, the engineer Schreiber added, "the darker the night, the brighter the stars."

As we were saying goodbye, Anna Samoïlovna Abramowicz passed me 300 rubles with the request that I pay the fine to have a family member released from prison.

I paid the fine. A week passed, then a second and a third. The arrested woman never appeared in the ghetto. Again, I went to the police. They explained that she had already been released. This was not true. I went to the women's prison. There they answered me that she had been shot dead long ago, and advised me, as a Lithuanian, not to make any further inquiries. I went directly to the police. There they told me to make myself scarce, or else I would be escorted to the German Gestapo. The money, of course, was never returned. The receipt had been issued for the release of a person known already to have been shot. (Šimaitė in Šukys, "And I burned" 65–66)

Anna did not survive. In September 1943 the Germans dispatched her to Treblinka, where she was killed. Dina was sent to a labor camp, but "by a stroke of fortune, the door on the cattle train opened on the Vilna platform and she simply walked off. She wound up in a less rigorous camp, one for workers who processed fur for the German army's winter coats," Kailis. "She escaped into the woods and joined Jewish resistance fighters as a nurse's helper" (Berger).

Šimaitė and Dina Abramowicz remained friends and correspondents until Šimaitė's death. Linked not only by the bond of the ghetto and war, the two women shared a love for libraries, archives, and the printed word.

[Abramowicz's] mind was a mental card catalogue for hundreds of rare and obscure books and historical materials. . . . When she came to New York in 1946, she soon went to work for the transplanted version of one of Vilna's most important institutions, the YIVO library, many of whose thousands of books and artifacts had been smuggled out by a ragtag band of slave laborers known as the paper brigade. (Berger)

In New York she joined her father, Hirsz Abramowicz, who in late June 1939 had left Vilnius for a two-month vacation in Canada and the United States. Instead of a tourist, Hirsz Abramowicz became a refugee, stranded in North America for the duration of the war.

In 1942 he suffered a heart attack, underwent a year of recuperation, then finally "began to respond to the terrible truth about the finality of the Holocaust and the harsh reality of living with this knowledge. . . . He wrote to commemorate, to bring to life those whose existence had been brutally cut off" (D. Abramowicz, "My Father's Life and Work" 29). Šimaitė, through her letters, was instrumental in giving him an image of how his wife and daughter had lived during the war years.

CHAPTER 21

Letters to New York

To Mr. Abramowicz, journalist and director of Vilna's Jewish Secondary School, who traveled to an international conference in New York, and stayed in America.[1]

APRIL 30, 1945

Mr. Abramowicz!
I don't know how quickly my letter will reach you, since I remember neither your new address, nor your daughter's in Paris, which was given to me before ghettoization by your wife. I hope that this letter reaches you, as I promised your wife Anna Samoïlovna that I would contact you.

My acquaintance with your family began in 1940. As an employee at Vilnius University library, I approached your daughter Dina, a librarian at the Jewish Children's Library, where there were Polish books, to ask permission to use them with my niece.

Dina was always exceptionally kind and attentive both to my niece and to me. Later in the ghetto, when I asked her about the reason for this positive attitude toward a complete stranger, I received a surprising response: "Anichka, there has never been a particularly good attitude toward the Jews in Vilna. I felt from the way you extended your hand . . ."[2]

From the very first day of the Nazis' arrival, it was hell for the Jews. The Jewish Children's Library was closed, like all other Jewish establishments, which were either closed or destroyed. . . .

September 6, 1941. The Jews were led into the ghetto. They could only take with them what they could carry. Even before the ghetto almost everything had been taken away from the Jews, or else plundered if they hadn't managed

141

18. Hirsz Abramowicz, 1934. YIVO Archives.

to take them to others for safekeeping. This happened to many people. The majority of those in power, for example, appropriated Jewish belongings. Jews couldn't complain, for complaints led only to the retort that they had handed these things over willingly.

September 14, 1941. I entered the ghetto, together with a co-worker from the university, Miss Godliauskaitė. I can't write about my first impressions of it. I will only tell you about your relations. Your wife and daughter lived in a single tiny room together with the entire Schreiber family and with the Zhazdik girls, who were much loved by the family (in all, 9 people). The furniture consisted of 1 bed, 1 table, 2 chairs. During the day all the bedding and belongings were piled into one corner. The floor was washed three times a day. It was very sad. Dina told me that, above all, she suffered from not being able to undress and bathe. Later, circumstances changed. The Jews built beautiful baths and arranged for all kinds of other necessary infrastructure.

A library was established in the ghetto soon thereafter and Dina was able to work in the library. But she didn't have a yellow "shayn." Only those with yellow shayns had the right to remain alive in the ghetto. Zhazdik, who worked at the German military office, had a yellow shayn and wrote Dina into it. He took her as his wife, even though he had a fiancée. The parents of the fiancée had yellow shayns, and so could "take" their daughter themselves.

Your wife was without any shayn until mid-January 1942. This was the most terrifying time, when people were constantly being taken away to their deaths, during the "cleansings." The first to be taken were those without shayns, then those with red or light blue shayns. During one of those "cleansings," when everyone, together with their families, was led out to the city to work, your wife ran away and hid at a woman's house on Subačiaus for two days, then in my apartment for four. In 1942 Froymchik, who worked for the ghetto courts, procured a yellow shayn for her.

Schreiber was an engineer who worked inside the ghetto all throughout ghettoization, and was able to get a yellow shayn. Out of nothing, he organized a technical school with electricians and other trades. Your wife was the cleaner in this school. Dina, who worked in the library, did this work instead. Dina helped her mother in every way possible, and always gave her the best piece of food. The poor ghetto food — bread and beans — was too heavy for Anna Samoïlovna. . . .

After the great "cleansing" of November 1941, your wife became calm, she no longer hid, and consciously decided not to resist the inevitable. She became very strong. . . .

She strove to become a pillar of support and calm not only for Dina, but for others too.

She dedicated every free moment to reading. For some reason, Dina only read French books in the ghetto. Anna Samoïlovna's favorite book in the ghetto was a volume of Bialik's poetry. She also read a great deal about black Americans, and was troubled to read how slaves eventually began to believe that they were of an inferior race.

There were beautiful concerts in the ghetto. Anna Samoïlovna attended them whenever she could.

Now we've come to April 5, 1943, when suddenly 5,000 people were supposedly taken away to work in Kovno, but in fact they were shot. It looked like the entire ghetto would be liquidated, so Anna Samoïlovna prepared a letter for you and your daughter who lives in Paris. I kept that and other letters, written by Dina and others, at my Vilna apartment. . . .

It was impossible to read your wife's letters without tears. She movingly said her farewells to you and your daughter. She was happy that you weren't in Vilna. She thanked you for all the good you had done her. She wrote that she considered herself to have lived an honest and good life. What she loved most in life, apart from you, were books, music, and flowers — these she had until her very last days. Once she grew tired, she decided not to keep struggling for a few more years of life. She asked you to mourn her. She said she would remember both of you in her final moments.

Two months before the liquidation of the ghetto, Dina left her position in the library. She began to work in a sawmill. It was painful to see her all white from sawdust. She advised everyone to try and find somewhere to run and hide. Alas, there was no such place to be found. During liquidation, Dina managed to escape against all odds.

Anna Samoïlovna didn't try to run. She had resigned herself to the Jewish lot.

Dina first ran to Julija [Šimaitė's sister], but there too she found no refuge there. Julija had done a great deal for your family . . . but she wouldn't risk her life for Dina. . . . From Julija's Dina ran to Kailis. But those who remained at Kailis, who had survived its liquidation (September 1–3, 1943), were also afraid. For every unauthorized Jew found there, ten would be killed. Despite this, Dina found shelter for a time at Kailis. Grisha Shur helped her collect warm clothes and join the partisans. I next received word about Dina from the forest on April 22, 1944, where she was with the Jewish Partisan detachment. Since she looked typically Semitic, she never left the forest, but stayed there to care for the sick. . . .

Forgive me, Mr. Abramowicz, that I can only tell you such unhappy things about your relatives.

I have a large favor to ask of you. I believe that the efforts of a friendly face might help me more than those of an organization in my attempts to inform others in America about loved ones. I don't know where they are, and I thought that you perhaps could help. . . .

If the opportunity presents itself, please, Mr. Abramowicz, give my regards to Prof. Shapiro, the lecturer in Ancient Hebrew and Arabic languages at Kaunas and Vilnius Universities. I've never forgotten his talk on new Palestinian literature. . . .

> *Be well, Mr. Abramowicz,*
> *Anna Šimaitė*

SEPTEMBER 9, 1945

Dear Mr. Abramowicz!

I was overjoyed to read that you address me as a "Dear Friend." This is how AS, your wife and powerful spirit, addressed me in her letters from the ghetto.

Your first letter took a whole month to reach me, I received it almost four weeks ago. The second reached me very quickly. I ask you to forgive me for not having replied sooner. I also have Jewish luck. Life is very difficult for me. But . . . I've recently had the opportunity to travel to a few places in France. This is why I haven't written for so long. You forgive me, don't you?

Your kindness touches me to the core. . . . Yes, I would very much like to have you as a friend, as I did AS and Dina.

I understand your wanting to thank me. But this is completely unnecessary. I simply fulfilled a promise to AS, whom I admired and loved. That's all. I appeal to you as a friend. I'm sure you will do whatever you can, but let it not be out of gratitude, all right? Indebtedness is a powerful sentiment, and I don't want you to have this feeling toward me. . . .

Since life in the camps I been working as a kitchen maid, first for 14–17 hours a day drying dishes, then 10–12 hours a day in another self-serve cafeteria, and I've had no time or energy to write down everything that I saw, that I encountered and experienced during the cannibalistic days. It's as if there's a large weight on my soul: the promises I made to my comrades — Gershon Malakiewicz, the Tzunzers, the Lichtensteins, the Trupianskis, and others who asked me to try to survive them and to tell EVERYTHING *to I. Steinberg about their tragic lives. And so, I thought I would not only write about them, but about other people in the ghetto, and not only about the Vilna Ghetto, but about the Kovno Ghetto and even Riga, where I traveled to learn about the fate of fellow Vilners, and to gather news and messages from them. It's necessary to tell about the enormous cultural life of the Vilna Ghetto. People there were grotesquely humiliated, and even so, a powerful culture was fostered. I would like to show the parallels between the cultural life in the Vilna Ghetto and in the rest of Vilna during the war years. . . .*

[I]f I work no more than 5–6 hours per day . . . I will write about all this to I. Steinberg. And you, together with Steinberg may do what you like with what I've already written. To these recollections must be added not only people you didn't know, but ones who were very close to you. I ask only one thing: that you not hurt the living. . . . You already know yourself what can be published and what can't.

In July I went to Paris for a few days, on an invitation from Doctor Marc Dworzhetsky. He is currently printing his memoirs of the concentration camps and the Vilna Ghetto in Dos Vort. *At first I had planned only to recount to Steinberg only what Dworzhetsky doesn't tell about the ghetto. But he talked me out of this. I might know something he doesn't. And, in general, we differ on certain facts. Doctor Dworzhetsky suggests that I write exactly as I like, and that it won't be a disaster if we write about the same facts. And he suggests that I send the text not only to Steinberg, but to the World Jewish Congress, to the American* yivo, *and to the rector of Hebrew University. I think that this is unnecessary. This kind of text would require a great deal of time. I think it will be enough for Steinberg to have the text, in addition to you and Friedman in Paris, who is the editor of the Socialist Worker's Newspaper. It's not a large newspaper, and some of these reminiscences could be printed there. . . .*

The botanist Y. Mowszowicz always urged me to keep notes. Alas, there was no time, and I considered that the most important things to write were texts (letters) that would make life easier for people. And Dina supported me in this. She considered the most important writings not to be chronicles (in the ghetto a few people were keeping these), but an evaluation of my experiences as a whole. I did write some things, but all that remained in Vilna. My memory is very good, with the exception of dates. In my letter to you I made a mistake regarding the liquidation of the ghetto. I've already corrected this in my letters to others. . . .

I'm including three more letters for you. Perhaps some of this will interest you. I've been unable to get M. Shur's address, no matter how hard I try. Could you write a letter in English to the newspaper the Zionist Record, *Johannesburg, South Africa, explaining that we are searching for Shur? Of course, the letter, which I've included for you was never sent to him. I was* told that he is very eminent and well-known by everyone. . . . Alas, I've never received any response. . . .

All of my Vilna "crimes" were committed out of love for Jewish culture and because I couldn't stand by and coldly watch the suffering of the Jews. . . .

Dina was terribly ragged in the ghetto. Few of your family's belongings were returned. I would also like to write about the "return" of Jewish belongings.

During the first winter in the ghetto . . . AS froze terribly without her felt boots. Over the course of 1½ months I sometimes went twice a day to try and retrieve the boots, but without success.

True, AS told me not to waste so much energy, but I like to finish what I start.

Because of malnutrition in the ghetto, many people suffered from boils and abscesses. AS suffered a great deal. Dina did too, almost continually. Just as one abscess healed, another would erupt. Life is very difficult in every place that has felt the winds of war. Vilna is no exception, and there's nothing more to be said about it.

How wonderful it would be if we could get Dina . . . out of there. . . .

Could you possibly try to have some diplomat intervene? At one time I worked among diplomats in Kaunas, and I know that small requests are sometimes fulfilled. . . . You should make it clear that you will pay all of Dina's transport costs, and that the USSR won't need to spend a cent.

I have no doubt that Dina wants to come to you or to her sister. Once in the ghetto she told me that even in the old days she never liked the streets of the medieval ghetto (the old town). With sadness she added that now she was being punished for that, and was forced to live there. Vilna is now a living cemetery. . . . I think that life there is very difficult for Dina.

When you write to Dina, please tell her that her friend Anya the librarian is in France. She will know who you mean.

I wrote a postcard about my fate to the university. Did it reach them? At the time of my release from the Soviet camp I gave the address of my relatives to one trustworthy woman. If possible, she will communicate to them in Lithuania from Latvia. I want my relatives, friends and comrades not to grieve, and to know that I'm alive. The Gestapo has paid compensation in the past and reunites people in such cases. Particularly since my friends were cheated out of the fine they paid several times for my release. . . . It was impossible to communicate with anyone from inside the camp. My heart hurts terribly from worry about my friends and comrades. Are they alive and well? . . .

It was impossible for me to keep the documents from the Vilna Ghetto.

They all stayed in Vilna. Soon you will receive a communication from Paris from Dr. Dworzhetsky about these documents and their location. In addition to you, Steinberg, Max Weinreich, and S. Weiss will also receive it. . . .

I've just received a letter from the Vilna Society ("Landsmannschaft") saying that they've received the poet Sutzkever's manuscript about Vilna (apparently, next month it will be published in Paris), in which he writes that I was killed by the Gestapo riflemen. He laments my death and the loss of the documents. This means that my loved ones don't know that I'm alive. The documents have not all been lost either. Of course, the editor will be notified that I'm alive.

What happened in Lithuania to both Jews and non-Jews remains an important question. But, above everything and everyone, the Jewish people suffered most. A few individual Jews miraculously survived. Yes, in my beloved Lithuania, such things occurred; events which are impossible to recall without terrible shame and spiritual torment. The Germans didn't shoot very many Jews themselves. They gave the orders to do so, and these were carried out by Lithuanians, Estonians (once the Germans lost trust in the Lithuanians), Ukrainians, and others. No matter who carried them out, my heart still shudders. Among the Lithuanians there was the "ypatingasis būrys" [special unit], under Norvaiša's command.[3] It specialized in the mass-shooting of Jews. To this group it's necessary to add the so-called ideological anti-Semites, various journalists (both Lithuanian and Polish), who wrote against Jews. . . .

You ask me why I mention Steinberg so often. Because he is the only light that I have left from my past life, before the Gestapo deprived me of everything. He is my spiritual teacher. I'm connected to him by the love of a student for a teacher. It is a special kind of love. It is radiant, good, and pure, when the thoughts and spirit of an author transfer to another person.

My friend, I understand very well the depth of your personal suffering and of your suffering as a son of the Jewish people. I would like to comfort you, but I don't have the appropriate words, for the suffering is too powerful. I know what that kind of suffering is, because I too have suffered and still suffer a great deal.

> *I wish you good health and ever more brightness in your life.*
> *A. Šimaitė*

CHAPTER 22

La Courtine

AUGUST 2007

Sebastian is six months old when we decide to travel from Toulouse to see Le Camp de la Courtine, where Šimaitė was interned after Ludelange. She has been slipping away from me over these past months. Despite my best intentions, fatigue and the demands of a new baby have made it impossible for me to visit with my ghostly friend the way I used to. I miss her terribly, so, even though it means that we will have to cross close to half of France, I'm determined to go.

The drive to La Courtine is awful. Sebastian screams for an hour. Sometime over the past eight weeks he has decided that he hates riding in the car. I find that I have horribly miscalculated the distances between the places I plan to see. It turns out that Šimaitė covered a lot of ground, and we will have to drive four hours each way to visit La Courtine. Sean still doesn't have a driver's license, so his job is to try and calm the baby while I take the wheel. It doesn't work very well, and by the time we reach the camp, the two of them are in a black mood. Even so, I'm still excited to see the camp.

We drive northward under an angry sky, but even under dark clouds, the Limousin glows green. We are heading to the Plateau des Millevaches, dairy country, and start to climb once we see signs for La Courtine. The forest around us grows thick, and begins to look increasingly northern, with its birches and old evergreens.

A military town, La Courtine is bigger than Ludelange, and has all the services of a real place. The houses here are made of stone and seem cold and forlorn in the rain. As we feel our way to the Military Camp, I'm surprised to find it is active. All around signs warn against unauthorized entry, so we return to the small museum, the "Maison de mémoire" at the camp's base. It is deserted, but inside a small display tells how Dutch soldiers helped the people of La Courtine through devastating floods in the 1960s. "I guess the Dutch know from floods," I say wryly to Sean. He's still angry, and only half-responds.

As I'm poking around the display, Thierry, an engineer and civilian employee of the army base returns. When I tell him that I have come to see the camp as part of my research on Ona Šimaitė, and ask if he knows anything about prisoners like her, he gets visibly excited. "Yes," he says. "Just last week an elderly couple came in. Both had been prisoners here in 1944. He was in the men's camp and she in the women's. They met here and eventually married. They were Belarusian." Šimaitė was probably interned with them. They had shown Thierry the barracks in which they had lived, and he could certainly show them to me. Otherwise, he tells me, there is little information on this fleeting period of the camp that marked the end of the Vichy regime — a time most people have preferred to forget. The prisoners of La Courtine were members of the anti-Nazi resistance, Belarusians, for the most part. During the year or so they spent there, they underwent a reeducation program. Most had been captive for four years and needed help reintegrating into society. Did they get French lessons? I ask. "Certainly," replies Thierry.

He has been waiting for a group of students to arrive from the military school. He will give them a tour of the Memory House, and a sense of the history of the camp. He can't give me a tour of the base, but will try to convince his wife to do so. I hear him arguing with her as he talks on his cell phone, telling her it will only

19. The barracks at Le Camp de la Courtine. Photo by author.

take a few minutes. She agrees and two minutes later she arrives in her car that is licensed to enter the base. As I climb in, I deduce from the bits of hay strewn about her vehicle that she and Thierry have horses. Sean and Sebastian will wait for me in our car while I take a quick tour.

The base's buildings are almost all stuccoed and color-coded. The barracks where Šimaitė would have been housed are now mint green. At the time she was interned here they almost certainly would have been plain stone. Two and a half stories each, with fourteen windows running down each side, the barracks are long and narrow. There is no vegetation around them, only gravel, so the straight lines and repetition from building to building, each one exactly the same, creates an impression of desolate and soul-killing tidiness. By holding up my camera right to the glass, I get a clear photo of a room where prisoners like Šimaitė underwent reeducation.

The drive back to Toulouse is wet and arduous. Sebastian cries and cries as we descend from the Plateau of the Thousand Cows, and only stops once we reach our stone house. As I put him to bed, I search the darkness for Šimaitė's familiar presence, but she is nowhere to be found. The tears have exhausted Sebastian, and his breathing relaxes into a heavy sleep. We are alone.

PART SEVEN

CHAPTER 23

The Ghetto Library

VILNA 1942

Herman Kruk lives at Number 6 Strashun Street, where the Judenrat and morgue are located. Carpenters build coffins in the courtyard outside his apartment. On May 19, 1942, this slight man, with dark hair and almond eyes, turns forty-five in the ghetto. "I shall get no flowers here — no one to give me anything," he writes in his diary. "I will not celebrate — there's nothing to celebrate. I bear my 45 years all alone, and especially the brand-new experiences from the 44th to the 45th" (Kruk, *The Last Days* 292). His forehead, broad and smooth in the prewar photograph will age a decade over the next two years.

He left Warsaw in September 1939 amid a throng of cars, bicycles, and pedestrians, traveling with five others by horse and wagon, and train. Bombs punctuated the men's journey through Poland, as did terrible news from Warsaw. Planes accompanied the group as it journeyed to Vilna through devastated villages and arrived only days before the Soviet invasion. All six men had left their wives behind, assuming the women would be safe (Harshav xlii). In Kruk's case, he left his second wife, a woman he married after the death of his first in childbirth. He never saw her again.

Two weeks after entering the ghetto, Kruk finds himself at the helm of an absurd yet strangely beautiful project: to create a haven of quiet, culture, and learning — a library. His office is out over the debris-littered courtyard, and it is here that Kruk dictates his letters and chronicle to his secretary, Rachel Mendelssohn. Typed in triplicate on long sheets of paper, single-spaced and dense, the chronicle is Kruk's most prized possession, the hashish of his ghetto life, as he puts it: "more than a thousand pages of woe, pain, and dread" (Kruk, *The Last Days* 324). Because of this chronicle, we know a lot about the reading habits and intellectual life of the Vilna Ghetto.

The space they have taken over had already been a library. The Enlightenment Library originally housed 45,000 books, but of these over 10,000 have gone missing, pillaged by both Germans and ghetto Jews. The card catalogue is gone too. A door in the library's lobby leads to a big, empty hall transformed to a reading room. Closed in 1925 for lack of funds, oddly it is under the conditions of the ghetto that the reading room's reopening becomes possible, its windows repaired, walls whitewashed, and boards collected for bookshelves. Half the reading room's books are fiction, and the other half periodicals and children's literature. Glass cabinets placed along the walls display Torah scrolls, silver wine cups, candle holders, and embroidered curtains for Torah arks. The library's collection grows to include sacred and valuable objects that people bring in hope of saving them. What accumulates is literally an embarrassment and tragedy of riches. Eventually the library staff will stop displaying new artifacts, since the destruction they attest to is too stark and terrible. The Torahs not on display will lie wrapped in bed sheets in the corner of the ghetto archive with public announcements, orders, reports, theater posters, and other paraphernalia stored for posterity. In this way, the ghetto librarians archive the destruction of their culture.

The library is among the first public institutions in the ghetto, and its first cultural establishment. It looks exactly as it did in former times, with clean floors freshly, impressive bookshelves, and unexpected serenity. In the first two weeks of the library's existence, there are already 1,500 members.

The initial functioning of the reading room is short-lived. It must close for several months because of cold weather and a typhus epidemic. But by September 1942, the library will have become the only building in the ghetto with central heating, fed by steam from a ghetto bath house.

A seven-day work week is put into effect. The library opens to the public from 10:00 a.m. to 7:00 p.m. Reading conditions are poor, as electricity is now restricted to 6:30 a.m. to 9:00 a.m. and after 9:00 p.m. Late-night reading is impossible because of the blackout order. Fines are imposed in the ghetto for burning lights or using kettles at forbidden times. When Kruk accidentally leaves a light on in the library office, there are calls for his arrest. The order is dropped only when friends intervene. But Kruk nonetheless extends the library's hours until 9:00 p.m. in the spring, as the northern days grow longer, with the summer sun setting only at 11:00.

Ghetto events have a major impact on the configuration of the library and on reading practices. Staff and readers alike are lost to mass deportations and executions called Aktions. Kruk observes a rise in readership following traumatic events. When on October 1, 1941, for example, 3,000 individuals are shot at Paneriai (Ponar), long lines form the next day to check out books. With each Aktion not only do readers disappear, but with them, books. Adult readers seek to be carried away to other places, times, and worlds. They read biographies and memoirs in great numbers, as well as Russian sentimental novels published in Riga. Light fiction, mysteries, and what Kruk calls "semi-trashy" books circulate widely. Even among intellectuals, he notes that there is little demand for classics. Exceptions are Tolstoy's *War and Peace*, Erich Maria Remarque's *All Quiet on the Western Front*, and Émile Zola's *War*. According to Dina Abramowicz in "The Library," Franz Werfel's *The Forty Days of Musa Dagh*, about the Armenian genocide of 1915, is the ghetto's most popular book. But children are the library's most avid and

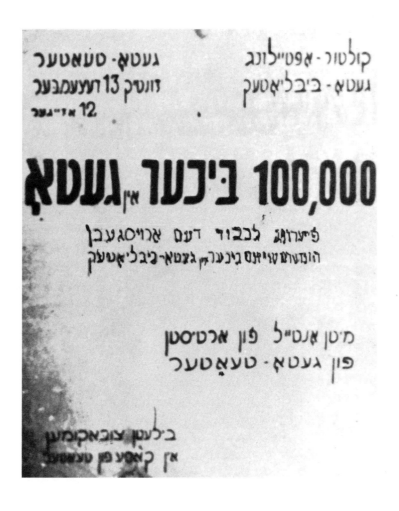

20. Vilna Ghetto poster informing of a celebration to mark the lending of 100,000 books by the ghetto library. Yad Vashem Archives.

voracious readers, exchanging books every day after school. Their texts are stained, greasy, and rebound so many times that the print runs into the gutter. Still, nothing deters the young readers.

By late November 1942 the library has lent a staggering 100,000 books. While Yiddish remains the language of the street and of the ghetto administration, not so the reading room and library. Seventy per cent of books here are read in Polish; Yiddish barely accounts for twenty per cent; Hebrew not even two. Russian reading, especially among older patrons, is on the rise as Polish books go missing, deteriorate, and as sets get broken up. On November 4, 1942, in an attempt to stem the tide of disappearing volumes, the ghetto library hands over to the ghetto police a list of delinquent borrowers. Alongside his role as librarian and archivist of the ghetto, Kruk tries to save as many precious texts as possible, handing over three thousand rare books from the Strashun library to the synagogue's courtyard janitor to hide. After the war, Šimaitė will describe his efforts, comparing him to:

a little mouse, gathering grains one by one for its nest, Herman Kruk himself brought and encouraged others to collect books in the ghetto....[1] It was amazing to see the consistency and patience with which he dug into the materials. When he came to the [university] library, he was always restrained, calm, and polite. Some university employees said: "When this little Jew with the yellow patches on his chest and his back comes to us — we want to stand up and bow our head to him." (Šimaitė qtd. in Harshav xlv)

In February 1942 Kruk is summoned by Alfred Rosenberg of the Rosenberg task force, together with two librarians, to sort books from the Strashun Library. To aid in the task they are provided with twelve workers with little understanding of the importance and cultural value of the texts they transport. They treat the books gruffly, carrying them like firewood. One tries to burn an illustrated Haggadah[2] to prevent Germans from seeing images of the Pharaoh whipping Jews.

21. Vilna, April 1943. Piles of books and papers at YIVO. Yad Vashem Archives.

Kruk's work for the Rosenberg Task Force affords him the privilege of circulating quite freely throughout the city, and among his numerous acquaintances at the university library is Šimaitė, whom he describes in his diary as "an elderly Lithuanian woman and a veteran social activist" (Kruk, *The Last Days* 138). Only forty-seven at the time, and hardly elderly, the ghetto has apparently taken its toll on her too.

Šimaitė's regular visits to the ghetto library are "rare bright moments in the gray, sad life [there]" (D. Abramowicz, "The Library" 169). When visiting the ghetto library, Šimaitė examines the shelves of Yiddish books, remarking that she would like to learn the language.

A large wooden table fills the room where the Task Force works. It is stacked high with books that Kruk and his colleagues sort. The poet Kazys Boruta and Šimaitė meet with the sorters regularly to take away texts to hide. But there are other witnesses to the destruction of Litvak literary heritage. Along the room's periphery, each from a curving, inverted triangle, an Ancient keeps vigil. The trompe-l'oeil in the room is breathtaking.

There is Plato, with his bald head and full beard. Archimedes sports a frown, perhaps in response to the scene unfolding below. Homer, who they say never really existed, but is the personification of an oral tradition, here has curls and a slightly bulbous nose. Diogenes looks disgusted and strong, his muscles impressively defined through line and shadow. Euripides, dignified and quiet, appears concerned. Aristotle, for his part, looks away. Heraclitus has a beautiful lion-like mane, but his eyes look empty, as if blinded by grief. Hesiod casts a heavier shadow than any of the others. Why? Anacreon we see only in profile, with a laurel wreath upon his head. Pindar looks straight ahead, pensive. Plutarch too. And finally Socrates, with his pug-nose, brings the room full circle.

Kruk arranges to have the task of selecting books for transport to Germany designated to him. Several important collections (from YIVO, the An-ski[3] Museum, the Children's Library, libraries of Jewish secondary schools, and the warehouse of the Kletzkin publishers) thus fall under his supervision. This allows him to select texts to smuggle into the ghetto and hide. The Strashun Library's collection has already been transferred to the university building. Also sent are Holy books from the Gaon's Prayer House and from the Old Prayer House located on the second floor opposite the Strashun Library. Built in 1440, the latter is home to countless rare books. Finally, texts from the Glaziers' Prayer House located at Number 9 Żydų, or Yidishe Street, have been sent there too. A month later Kruk sets up a secret warehouse for artifacts that Rosenberg doesn't know about including: thousands of holy books (some dating to the fifteenth century), more than 200 Torah Scrolls, cantors' pulpits, ark coverings, and art. He smuggles much of this into the ghetto by hiding it inside furniture.

When Kruk visits the Yiddish Institute YIVO later in March 1942, he finds everything in disarray. Cards from the catalog lie on the floor in mounds, and beneath them lie paintings and other works of art. The elements of the Y. L. Peretz exhibition, held in 1940–1941, have been torn down and thrown into an attic. Manuscripts and pictures are mixed with sand, so Kruk's first order of business is to save these materials. With the whole building at his disposal, here too he will collect rare books. A few days later a child is spotted playing with glasses in the ghetto. They belonged to the writer Peretz. Treasures are now almost routinely found in the filth of the ghetto — a letter from the Vilna Gaon is retrieved from the gutter of Ghetto II.

Among the ruins of the Small Ghetto Kruk finds two vials of strychnine. Combining these with three others already in his possession, he is ready for anything.

But he will not use this poison. The Germans will transport him, together with thousands of others, to the labor camps of Klooga and Lagedi in Estonia to build a defense wall. On September 18, 1944, like so many others, he will be tied up, ordered to lie down on a pyre, shot, then set ablaze. His diary will be recovered by the only surviving witness to its burial.

CHAPTER 24

Librarians

LIBRARIANS care for our memories and our histories. They catalog the dreams we never knew we had, do not let us forget the transgressions of the past, and safeguard our stories of love, loss, and redemption. They are keepers of the human soul. This is why we cry when libraries burn. When a library is destroyed, so are we. Šimaitė understood this. To her, as to every librarian, the library stood for life itself. And under her care the Vilnius University stacks and archives became a repository for life. I reconstruct her story, sifting the mundane from the extraordinary, and searching for the exquisite in the everyday, unearthing buttons and other brass treasures buried decades ago.

The dead accompanied Šimaitė throughout her life in the form of whispering ghosts and unwritten texts. For more than eight years Šimaitė has accompanied me in similar form. She is the voice of my own unwritten text, and she comes with me to libraries, appears in my dreams, watches over me, and walks beside me on my travels. She and I circumnavigated the globe together, my box of photocopied letters growing heavier with each archive visited, until I could no longer carry it onto the plane and was forced to check it as baggage.

Is it death that draws women to libraries? To become librarians? Or writers?

When I begin to read about Šimaitė's beloved profession, I despair at what I find. Rather than a rare space where women call the shots as appears to be the case in the Vilnius University Library today, libraries, and especially academic ones, most often operate on a "harem" model, where men lead and women facilitate their work, toiling at their sides.[1] This was certainly true of Vilnius University Library when Šimaitė worked there. Vaclovas Biržiška, the university rector's brother, was the library director and all around him — the women of the library.[2]

All the usual discrepancies hold in the economy of the library: women earn less than men, receive promotions less frequently, and hold fewer positions of authority. Library hierarchies, it seems, have developed according to assumptions about women's competencies and interests, perhaps most notably in the case of the cataloger. Cataloging requires attention to detail and the endurance of boredom, repetitive work, and even pain — characteristics traditionally considered to be feminine.

So, here's the rub: slowly my brave, revolutionary librarian is being transformed for me as I read. I get a sinking feeling when I realize that not only did she work within a harem structure, but that she was a *cataloger*, the lowest of the low. The most repetitive, unprestigious position reserved for women and our fiddly little talents. I realize too that she probably earned about half of what her male colleagues did, though she probably worked harder. And although she treated her job as a vocation and considered libraries sanctuaries, maybe she only worked among books because to her, as a woman, it was one of the few avenues open to her. Perhaps, I suddenly realize, my affection for her has started to blind me. To what extent do I not see what I don't like?

The risk here, despite my earlier pronouncement that she would have made a good saint, is hagiography. I promised Kęstutis Šimas, Šimaitė's nephew, that I wouldn't canonize her. "No," he said. "She would have hated that." I must be careful.

CHAPTER 25

Writing a Woman's Life

WHY have women traditionally written so little when compared with men? And what needs to change in women's lives in order to make writing possible? Why have women been so absent from literary history? The answer, Virginia Woolf tells us in *A Room of One's Own*, lies in the conditions of women's lives. Women raise children, have not inherited wealth, and have had had fewer opportunities to make the money that would buy time for writing. Women rarely have partners who cook and clean and carry (or share equally) the burden of home life. Our lives have traditionally been and largely continue to be fractured, shared between childcare, kitchen duties, family obligations. To write, what a woman needs most is private space (a room of one's own), money, and connected time (that only money can buy). Woolf wrote her thoughts on women and writing in the 1920s and '30s, a time before all the ostensibly labor-saving devices like washing machines, slow cookers, microwave ovens, dishwashers, and so on. Most North American women now work outside the home, and most can probably find a corner in their houses to call their own. Problem solved? No. Despite all this, we still find ourselves fractured and split.

As it turns out, Šimaitė and I are not alone. We are part of a larger project: a rethinking of women's lives and of how to write them that began with Virginia Woolf.

Until now, I've been reading Šimaitė's writing and lack of completed memoirs in terms of trauma. That is, that she didn't write her memoirs because she couldn't face the past and obsessively wrote letters as a way of avoiding the real task at hand. And although I still believe this to be partially true, Woolf points to a much simpler explanation for the lack of memoirs: poverty. Šimaitė was poor, and therefore spent a huge proportion of her waking hours doing odd jobs, chasing paid work, tracking down debts, paying off debts, following up on promised pensions, writing letters justifying her continuing need for a pension, and so on. Was Šimaitė, then, a writer *manqué(e)*, a scribe lost to economics? Another potential woman of letters lost to poverty, as Virginia Woolf suggests?

Writing a woman's life as a woman. To respect not only one's subject's methods of inscribing the dailiness of her life, but to respect one's own voice. Years ago I began to think of myself as having a relationship with Šimaitė, and I imagined my research in the archives as a conversation. She spoke to me through her diaries and letters, and I responded to her through my writing. As a result, my understanding of Šimaitė's life is inextricably linked to the experience of my own.

Šimaitė lived through reading and writing. It was a major struggle for her to clear the time she needed to accomplish the literary work she both desired and felt obligated to do. And now, as my own life fills increasingly with thankless everyday tasks, I find I understand her more and more. As I get older, counting off year after year, I too feel the march of time and lament wasted hours as she did. I understand her frustration because I too am frustrated. I understand her loneliness when I too feel lonely. And I follow her in my imagination because I trust her as a guide to her personal past. I interpret the signs she leaves, I fill in the gaps as best I can, but I cannot claim to know. Where I invent, I must admit it. Because I do not want to lie to my reader, or to betray my friend Šimaitė, I cannot erase myself.

The first year and a half of my son's life shattered my understanding of myself as a writer. Only after making a series of unilateral decisions about childcare, home care, and food supply did I begin to claw back writing time and relocate a sense of my former identity. I was angry that my work always came last on the list of priorities: after laundry, meal preparation, house cleaning, shopping, and so on. And I was lonely, so, like Šimaitė or Dina Abramowicz would have done, I went to the library to look for community. I found Virginia Woolf. Not original, I know, but reading her words some ninety years after she wrote them, I felt a deep sense of kinship. There's a scene in *A Room of One's Own* where Woolf is turned away from a library because women are not allowed inside. Her outrage resonated in me. Even after the publication of books and articles, after lectures and grants, a message continues to be subtly communicated. Writing is not real work, and women who write are tolerated — still, how many years after Woolf? — until their real lives begin. That is, until they have children.

In "Professions for Women" Woolf coined the phrase "killing the Angel in the House," pointing to it as what women writers (or at least this woman writer) needed to do to keep on being writers. Who is the Angel? She is sympathetic, charming, unselfish, family-focused, self-sacrificing, undesiring, compliant, and generous. "Had I not killed her," Woolf writes, "she would have killed me. She would have plucked the heart out of my writing" (Woolf, *Women and Writing* 59).

Even before I'd come across Woolf's words, I'd embarked on the process of killing the Angel in my own House. The road was bumpy, but the Angel is dead. I'm writing again. I'm talking to Šimaitė once more. I feel her presence, and for the first time in a long while, I'm not angry.

Though Šimaitė was unmarried and raised no children, she too felt the weight of the Angel in the form of unanswered letters, unpaid debts, and a home that she could never clean to her satisfaction. The Angel took its toll on her. Her promised memoirs remained unwritten and spiritual flame began to fade.

With fifteen years of life still left to live, Šimaitė was tired. Her desire to work began to wane:

JUNE 8 [1955]

I don't have the words to describe how I suffered today from the heat, and they say it isn't even particularly hot today. My spirit is suffering from my inability to work. I can't even understand what I read anymore. The desire to strive is dying. My soul is starting to die! (Diary 8)

PART EIGHT

CHAPTER 26

Aldutė

THE final piece: Šimaitė's family letters.

When I went to Vilnius in 2006 Šimaitė's nephew Kęstutis gave me permission to look at the family's collection at the university archives. When he was a boy, Šimaitė had tromped around Paris for days looking for the "cowboy pants" he was dying for. Šimaitė had two sisters, Julija (whom she called Julė or by the diminutive Julytė, as my ninety-eight-year-old grandmother still calls me) and Liudmila (Liuda), as well as a brother, Kazys, Kęstutis's father. There are also letters from their spouses and children among the files. Having imagined I would whip through the letters in a matter of days, I was stunned by the beauty, tragedy, and complicated record of love that these letters constituted. Kęstutis had once told me that the whole Šimas clan was idiosyncratic, not only his aunt Šimaitė. It quickly became clear how true this was.

If the letters attest to anything, it's to the fact that Šimaitė's family had no shortage of tragedy. In a single family we encounter tales of arrest, university expulsion, prison, deportation, torture, exile, death by cancer, and by starvation. And yet, almost all the family letters refer at some point to Šimaitė's niece Aldutė and her troubles.

If the loveliest piece of Šimaitė's correspondence is her affectionate wartime exchange with the poet Kazys Jakubėnas, it is her letters to and from her niece Aldutė that are its most devastating.

Šimaitė's exchange with Aldutė, Aldutė's mother Julija, her father Pranas, friend Tayda, cousin Aldona, and husband Sasha took place over almost a decade: from 1959 to 1968. Slowly as I read, letter by letter, the tragedy unfolds before me. At its center stands Aldutė, a mentally ill woman trapped in a totalitarian society. All around her the family crumbles under pressure, and on the periphery of the inner circle, there is suicide, poverty, threat of arrest, and despair.

If these letters reveal anything about Šimaitė, it is her compassion for the anguished and her facility for forgiveness. Only after a decade of poisonous letters from her sister and niece do the first hints of bitterness creep into her diary entries. She defends Sasha, Aldutė's outcast husband, when all others have written him off as good for nothing, and advocates time and time again for an understanding of the mentally ill. Surrounded as she was by death, madness, dementia, and despair in her last years at the nursing home at Cormeilles, perhaps she empathized with Aldutė even more acutely.

On the day of her Vilnius arrest by the Gestapo in April of 1944, Šimaitė's niece, with whom she had plans to go to the theater, arrived at her aunt's apartment only to find an SS soldier waiting for her. She too was arrested and interrogated for three days. What horrors sixteen-year-old Aldutė may have suffered we do not know, but eight years after this arrest symptoms of mental illness began to surface.

As voracious a reader (reading "is the greatest source of solace, calm and form of medicine in my life" [Šimaitė, letter to Aldutė Stasionytė, October 2, 1959, Šimaitė's Papers, Vilnius University]) and producer of letters as she was, Šimaitė was of course serious about the epistolary form. Writing to Aldutė, she impressed upon her the solemnity with which she approached her correspondence:

OCTOBER 20, 1959
The great German poet [Rainer Maria] Rilke has said that one needs to write a letter as if saying a prayer: concentrated, and with bells ringing. Even though no bells are ringing, it's as if I see you before me, my dearest.

22. Aldutė as a student. Vilnius University Library Rare Books and Manuscripts Department.

Yes, I am saying a prayer, that you may have more moments of sunshine. . . .
And to ask that you, my Aldutė, might endure the unendurable. (Šimaitė's
Papers, Vilnius University)

But Aldutė's letters to Šimaitė and the letters of her family, simultaneously narrating and silencing her illness, tell us a story that's worth listening to. They communicate the experience of a woman living with the diagnosis of schizophrenia in the USSR in the 1950s and 1960s — not as a dissident or intellectual, but as someone small, vulnerable, and lonely. How does a victim of multiple powers represent herself to the outside world? And how do those who love her (in their own ways, for better or for worse) represent her?

The letters from family members, including Aldutė's mother, father, and cousin, give us information about her pharmaceutical regime. We know for example that she is taking Largactil, one of the first drugs used to treat schizophrenia, and that Aldutė is inconsistent with her drug regime. We witness, through letters, the strain on Aldutė's parents' relationship, and watch as their marriage breaks down. But these, whether from Aldutė herself or other family members, record nothing of her specific symptoms or behaviors, and give no real portrait of her illness. On November 28, 1962, Šimaitė responds to an upsetting letter from Aldutė who rails against her family:

I keep waiting for you to write and tell me what happened, and what is weighing so heavily on your aching soul? There's a saying that after sharing your troubles, you'll only be left with half of them. . . . Tell me the facts. What happened? . . . It's difficult to talk to you, Aldutė, because you don't write facts, but use vague words of pain. Tell me more specifically. Then I'll be able to give you my opinion. (Šimaitė's Papers, Vilnius University)

The temptation to pathologize Aldutė and to read her letters as the ravings of a sick mind is strong. But it seems to me that the richness of this collection-within-a-collection lies in its uncertainty. Whom do we believe? Where does the truth lie? Whether Aldutė's or her family's vagueness results from a concern for privacy, protection, or a sense of shame is unclear, but it forces the reader to consider each correspondent's version of Aldutė on its own terms. We cannot simply write off Aldutė's worldview as pathological, for who is to say that the accusation that her mother poisoned her marriage is unfounded? Plenty of marriages have been harmed by meddlesome in-laws, and how can we know that this is not the case here? How can we identify a delusion in the absence of certainty? With each letter the ground shifts as new doubts displace former ones.

CHAPTER 27

Family Letters

ON October 1, 1956 Šimaitė's sister Julija writes her a letter. It is the first word that the librarian has received from her family since her 1944 arrest in Vilnius. In it Julija delivers the blow that all is not well at home:

My dear Onutė!
I'm so happy that you are alive and well. All this time I thought you were dead. But happiest of all was my Aldutė.
 Onutė, I have some terrible news. My Aldutė is not very well. We don't know what to do. She started going downhill four years ago, and I don't know how to help her. We've been to see all kinds of doctors, but nothing helps. . . . She's had a lot of problems that she still hasn't gotten over, and she's all alone in the world. . . . Maybe if she had someone to go out with, she could forget her troubles. She was studying medicine, but didn't like it . . . and only barely finished six courses. She didn't write the state exams, because she couldn't and can't study or work. The nerve specialist, Žiugžda, recommended that we take her to Leningrad's psychiatric institute to see if they would accept her for treatment, but she refuses to go . . . and won't hear any more about it. She takes drugs (barbiturates) to sleep . . . and we're all going out of our minds. . . . I don't know what to do to help Aldutė, because she's going to die.
 Julija
 (Julija Stasionienė, Šimaitė's Papers, Vilnius University)

For her part, Aldutė is lucid and candid about her psychological difficulties in her first letters. On December 14, 1956, she writes,

176

"My dear Auntie! . . . I've been having a hard time recently, which is why I haven't written for so long. . . ." And on September 30, 1959, she offers an apology: "My dear Onelė! . . . Forgive me for writing so little, because my hand is writing badly from the meds" (Aldona Stasionytė, Šimaitė's Papers, Vilnius University). The river of information flowing westward about her behavior and healing regime does not escape Aldutė. By 1959, only three years into their correspondence, she complains to Šimaitė that her family is robbing her of her voice by speaking for or over her.

July 20, 1959
There's such a large chorus singing on my behalf that no one can even hear my voice. I don't know who's been singing to you over there. It's just too bad that there isn't a single person I love among those singers. . . .

I must say I'm surprised that so many people like to write about me, and I'd just like to say one thing: if people only talked about what they knew, silence would rule the world. . . .

I feel like I've been buried alive — so what can I hope for . . . take pleasure in? I can only be happy!!! Yes, I'm very happy to have everyone point and call me a madwoman. Oh yes, I'm very happy. And it's a pleasure to listen to the chorus of people who degrade me with cruelty. . . . Forgive me for this letter. It's not a very pleasant one for a name day.
  All the best.
  Aldutė
(Aldona Stasionytė, Šimaitė's Papers, Vilnius University)

Through the letters written by her mother, cousin, and father, we learn of Aldutė's addiction to barbiturates, of her loneliness, her inability to get out of bed for days at a time, her inability to work, lax hygiene, aggression, and anger. Through all of it, Šimaitė's letters keep flowing and carrying the same message: forgive, understand, forgive. She writes frankly yet compassionately to Aldutė about her mental health, beseeching her in one heartbreaking letter to try to wean herself from the drugs she uses to sleep:

I wanted to ask you, beg you to stop using the Barbamil. On nights when you can't sleep, try to use a little less each time. Don't go on killing yourself, Aldutė, my darling. I'm down on my aching arthritic knees, begging you. You have to help yourself, never forget that. No one else can help you. Help yourself, my dearest. You have to be strong and beat the unbeatable. Remember that there are situations when drugs are not available, as was the case when I was in the concentration camp. People are forced to endure the unendurable. Try to endure willingly. Don't be angry, don't be offended by what I write. We've agreed to be open about everything. Don't think, Aldutė, that I don't understand what kind of superhuman heroism I'm asking of you. (October 20, 1959, Šimaitė's Papers, Mažvydas)

But the open tone of the letters does not last. By 1959 Julija has begun to police all contact with Aldutė and to censor the content of their letters, which she believes upsets and harms her daughter:

MARCH 16, 1959

Onutė, please don't write anything about Aldutė's health in your letters, because she gets very agitated and feels terrible afterward. Then it's very difficult for us too. . . . Don't remind her of the past either, because the memories upset her terribly. . . .

She's already twenty-nine years old, and her emotions have become too much for her. I think she's suffered a heartache that she can't forget. Perhaps it would have been different had she married. Don't write to her about any of this, or else she'll be on me about every word. . . . If you want to write something, send it to [Aldutė's cousin], and she'll hand-deliver it to me.

Julė

(Julija Stasionienė, Šimaitė's Papers, Vilnius University)

Marriage in 1961 and the birth of Aldutė's son in 1962 seem to bring on a permanent shift in her mental health. Whereas until then, Šimaitė had been her one real confidante, about four months after the birth of the baby, Aldutė begins to sabotage their relationship, returning letters unread and torn up. Their correspondence ends in 1963, seven years before Šimaitė's death, with the following series of parting shots fired by Aldutė:

You don't know, for example that your . . . little maniac is often forced to spend the night at the station — and that she sleeps calmly . . . and returns home only because she can't take her little boy with her. If I didn't tell you this, you would never know. Just as you don't know so many other things. But I'm happy. (Aldona Stasionytė, undated letter, 1963, Šimaitė's Papers, Vilnius University)

As for you, I don't know how to start. I'll just say that you have no under-standing of me, of my life, or of life in the Soviet Union. . . . As someone who once worked for Soviet diplomats, and who sympathizes with the proletariat, you should have a better understanding of life in a Soviet country. I'm afraid you're under the influence of bourgeois propaganda. . . .

You don't know my life at all, you don't know my views or anything — and it's my own fault. It's my fault that I remained silent while others did the talking. (Aldona Stasionytė, July 1, 1963, Šimaitė's Papers, Vilnius University)

And finally:

I read your letter again and understood that you were mocking me because of my illness. Is that really so? It would be interesting . . . to know why. If this is true, then of course I'm very grateful to my loved ones. I'm just wondering if it's true. It would make things easier for me if I knew.

I would be grateful if you answered this letter. (Aldona Stasionytė, undated letter, 1963, Šimaitė's Papers, Vilnius University)

CHAPTER 28

Soviet Schizophrenia

WHEN I started to read about schizophrenia and its treatment in the USSR, I immediately found myself confronted by a couple of thorny issues. The first was the diagnosis and definition of schizophrenia itself. What Soviet psychiatrists considered to be schizophrenia was not necessarily held as such elsewhere in the world. The second difficulty I had to face was the issue of Soviet punitive psychiatry in the USSR: the diagnosing and treatment of political dissent as mental illness.

A 1973 World Health Organization study found that two countries differed significantly in their definition of what constituted schizophrenia from the eight other countries studied. One was the United States, where bipolar disorder was long diagnosed as schizophrenia, and the other was the USSR, where psychiatry employed a broad conception of the illness and categorized it using a unique system. The system's inventor, Shnezhnevsky, identified three forms of schizophrenia: continuous (progressive deterioration, without remission, and with no possibility of recovery), shift-like (attacks and remissions, but with eventual degeneration), and periodic (whereby a normal personality is attacked by delusions, but where full recovery is possible) (Bloch and Reddaway 246–47). This last category opened the door to the diagnosis of schizophrenia in the absence of symptoms (and in the presence of "seeming normality") and to punitive psychiatry: the diagnosing of political or religious dissenters and dissidents with mental illness, confining them in mental hospitals and treating them with psychotropic drugs (Bloch and Reddaway 249).

In *Russia's Political Hospitals*, Sidney Bloch and Peter Reddaway quote the Russian psychiatrist V. M. Morozov as saying "It's no secret to anyone that you can have schizophrenia without schizophrenia" (257). Clinical criteria used by forensic psychiatrists for the diagnosis of schizophrenia in dissenters included: "paranoid reformist delusional ideas," an "uncritical attitude toward his [or her] abnormal condition," "opinions having a moralizing character," the "over-estimation of his [or her] own personality," and "poor adaptation to the social environment" (Bloch and Reddaway 251). Lithuanian dissenters forcibly committed to mental institutions included Vytautas Grigas, interned in 1974 after taking part in a demonstration demanding the right for ethnic Germans to emigrate; Petras Cidzikas, interned in 1973 for circulating *samizdat* literature; and Birutė Poškienė whose husband turned her over to the authorities in 1974 after she converted to Protestantism and became a vegetarian. Doctors demanded that she renounce Protestantism to be released, but there's no information on whether or not they required her to eat meat to prove her mental soundness.

Phyllis Chessler argued in her 1972 book *Women and Madness* that: "Most women who are psychiatrically hospitalized are not 'mad.' Rather than challenge the psychophysical vocabulary of the female condition, they adopt its tone more surely than ever. They are depressed, suicidal, frigid, anxious, paranoid, phobic, guilty, indecisive, inactive, and without hope" (Chessler 164). To be sure, Aldutė is unhappy, lonely, and addicted to narcotics ("ex-patients ... exhibited many 'feminine' behaviors, such as fatigue, insomnia, pill-taking, and general 'inactivity'" [Chessler 51]), but her letters and those surrounding her illness are vague and discreet enough that we do not really know if it included classic symptoms of schizophrenia, like auditory hallucinations or so-called word salad. The language and reasoning in her letters make sense. In some she even employs writerly techniques, repeating in one instance the word "išėjau" (I went out), rhythmically like a mantra as she tells how she escaped from her parents' apartment to look for some peace and ended up having a meal in a local cafeteria. She ends the passage with a deft switch to "įėjau" (I went into), achieving a subtle repetition with a difference and a nice poetic apogee:

FEBRUARY 22, 1963

I got up with a great weight pressing into my chest, and with a slight head-ache. From my eyes fell tears upon remembering the past few days and upon seeing my surroundings. What to do? I got dressed and went out. I went out knowing that things would be bad at home, that I would end up running around searching for a cup that was right in front of me, and that the beast would mock me, asking me why I'm so screwed up.... I went out, though if I'd woken up cheery and content, while [the baby] slept I could have done some of the work that's been piling up all around. I went out knowing that [the baby] is still nursing almost exclusively, even though he should be getting a variety of foods by now. I went out early, at 8:00 a.m., looking for calm. I went into a cafeteria and bought a big breakfast so I wouldn't get hungry for a long time, and maybe I'd make it all the way to lunch — I don't want to eat anything at home, where mother gives every person she meets on the street an accounting of how her daughter is eating her out of house and home. (Aldona Stasionytė, Šimaitė's Papers, Vilnius University)

But if there is one classic symptom of schizophrenia that even I can detect in Aldutė's letters, it is paranoia: "schizophrenic patients believe that they are persecuted, watched, hypnotized against their will, and interfered with" (Smith 31) — and there's the rub. Can you be considered paranoid if your suspicions are true? Aldutė *rightfully* feels watched, judged, discussed. Every letter that travels from Vilnius to Paris contains an anecdote, observation, or pronouncement about the crazy one in the family. Aldutė *justifiably* characterizes this as a chorus of voices that drowns hers out. Evidently, Šimaitė too found it so hard to sort out fact from fiction that she began to send envoys — prewar friends and correspondents — to check on Aldutė in person, then send back reports. Most often dispatched on family information gathering missions is Vytautas Kauneckas, the Translator, who also has a daughter diagnosed with schizophrenia. As if his daughter's mental illness weren't enough to contend with, the Translator's short biography offered by Šimaitė in her diary can leave no doubt that he has had more than his fair share of hardship:

JUNE 24, 1959
I receive very sad letters from Dr. V. K., the former Vorkuta inmate. He spent eight years in the gulag. There was a revolt. He was shot in the coal mine. After those eight years, he spent another two in hospital. He's now deaf in one ear, and is lame. For a long time Madam Secret Police wouldn't leave him alone. The man has born everything, and nothing has broken him. Now he complains of swelling in his legs, and all kinds of difficulties with transla- tions, whereas he's the one who translated Darwin and The Little Prince . . . for them. Now he hasn't a crumb to eat, because no book is acceptable to their ideology. (Diary 22)

On September 10, 1968, the Translator sent the following report:

I wanted to respond to your letter about Aldutė, so I'll at least jot down a few of my thoughts here. . . . Il faut essayer d'y voir clair (we must try to see things clearly), as the French say. The situation has become complicated mostly because there's no hope of reaching an agreement with Aldutė. I think that neither Alfonsas [Jakubėnas] nor I would succeed in talking to her: she's ill; she flies off the handle at the drop of a hat; logic doesn't work on her. If she won't hand over the child willingly, then he has to be taken from her by force. The child's interests have to come first. But there's no way she'll give up her kid willingly; and if her parents take him . . . then she'll show up, make a scene, and the whole thing will spiral out of control. But she won't come if she's in a home or hospital. But the way she's living now — with no income, not eating regularly, not sleeping at night — she can't go on like that for much longer: if only for her own good, it looks like (unfortunately), she's headed for hospitalization. . . . Your sister seems to think that Aldutė is full of ill will and stubbornness. But her behavior is probably due to her illness, unconscious, and beyond her control. (Vytautas Kauneckas, Šimaitė's Correspondence, Hoover)

Based on the letters that she received from Vilnius, Šimaitė must have had the impression that the city she loved had become a madhouse. In addition to stories about Aldutė and Kauneckas's daughter, she got reports that her sister Julija was on the edge of a breakdown, that her other sister's husband was a paranoiac, and that her youngest brother was just plain mad. Finally, the last straw came with the news that one of her correspondents, a successful female editor at Lithuania's State Literary Publishing House who sent her Lithuanian books, had committed suicide out of the blue one day at the age of thirty. If even someone so rooted in and well treated by the Soviet machine couldn't survive, then what hope did poor Aldutė have?

Ričardas Gavelis's 1989 novel *Vilnius Poker*, set in the 1970s, presents a city where the only sane worldview is that of a conspiracy theorist and paranoiac. "Vilnius pants convulsively like a dying beast" and "sprawls helplessly, almost paralyzed, its hands shackled and its mouth gagged" (Gavelis 26). As in Šimaitė's family correspondence, uncertainty reigns in this Vilnius as well: each of the novel's four narrators is unreliable, giving a different version of the same murder. The novel challenges the reader, forcing her to ask who is telling the truth? Vytautas Vargalys poses a very simple question: who's crazy now? And he suggests that in Vilnius circa 1971 perhaps paranoia is the new reasonable. Perhaps the crazy ones — aren't:

A hundred times I tried to logically refute Their *existence. But I reached the opposite goal — I unarguably proved that* They *really exist. . . . who raises and sets all governments on the throne, who hands the scepter to Satan's servants — to all sorts of Stalins, Hitlers or Pol Pots? How do thousands, even millions of people disappear in the presence of all, and the others supposedly don't even notice? (Gavelis 57)*

In a letter dated October 2, 1959, Šimaitė tells Aldutė about a documentary film called (loosely translated) "Rendezvous with the Devil" that tells the story of communities living close to active volcanoes: "They said that people who live close to such volcanoes don't philosophize, but take life as it is. I like that idea. I'd like for you, my dearest Aldutė, to accept life without self-hatred, and as it is, but with the hope that the day will come when things will get better." In other words, *They* might be out there (whether *They* are the regime, the voices inside, or the uncontrollable impulses), but life must be lived with all its suffering, and it must be done so with gratitude and joy and forgiveness. "No, Aldutė, there is no evil in you. There's just great pain. In your place, even an angel could have turned malicious. . . . Never forget, Aldutė, that there is an Onuška in this world who loves and will love Aldutė, even if she becomes malicious and badly behaved. Even bad you would be no less precious to me than you are when you are good" (Šimaitė's Papers, Mažvydas).

Chessler asked of American women institutionalized in the 1960s: "Are these women 'sick'? Are they more 'sick and tired' than medically 'sick'?" (72). It seems to me that it's worth at least asking the same question of Aldutė, and to entertain Šimaitė's suggestion. Is she really sicker than any of us might have been in her shoes?

CHAPTER 29

Death in Vilnius

STORIES within stories. Šimaitė's life story contains the traces of other lives, perhaps as every life story does. She herself understood this. Šimaitė believed that some of these stories were in danger of dying with her, and so she ensured that her Paris correspondence would be archived to save them. In turn, her correspondents in Israel and Lithuania kept the letters they received. Among them we have Aldutė the schizophrenic, Kazys the slain poet, Kauneckas the dictionary maniac. And we must now add Tayda Devėnaitė, the suicidal editor.

A reader and book lover, Devėnaitė rose quickly to a position of influence in the world of Lithuanian publishing while still in her early twenties. She began corresponding with Šimaitė in 1957, when preparing an edition of the collected works by the poet Salomėja Nėris, a late, prewar friend of Šimaitė. She tracked down Šimaitė in Paris to ask for help with the edition. "Perhaps you have some of Salomėja Nėris's manuscripts, letters, or other material?" she wrote on April 1, 1957 (Šimaitė's Papers, Vilnius University). The letter sparked a long affectionate correspondence. Šimaitė shared memories about Nėris and others, and even visited the places the poet had lived in Paris. Devėnaitė for her part sent Šimaitė streams of books. Unlike most of her correspondents in Vilnius who eked out lives on tiny pensions and miniscule wages, sharing cramped quarters with family members, Devėnaitė was part of the Soviet establishment. She had a large apartment all to herself, a princely salary of 1,200 rubles per month, and was free to travel in Eastern Bloc countries like Bulgaria, Hungary, and neighboring Soviet republics.[1] But despite her privilege and relative wealth, even Devėnaitė occasionally needed material help. Šimaitė used to send her heart medication to pass on to the poet Janina Degutytė, whose poem "Undeliverable Letters" reads: "I build homes with poems / I have nothing else to give." Ever conscious of not taking advantage of her friend's kindness, Devėnaitė wrote on April 10, 1959:

These medications are very expensive, and you've deprived yourself of many things to buy them. I don't know how to thank you. . . . The poet is feeling much better. Her collection "Fire Drops" has come out. Bookstores sold out of it immediately. (Šimaitė's Papers, Vilnius University)

Šimaitė saw an opportunity to try and help her suffering Aldutė by hooking her up with Devėnaitė, both privately and professionally. Devėnaitė was only too happy to help, and used her influence and money to provide Aldutė with travel documents for Leningrad and the Caucasus, where she met her husband Sasha. Šimaitė repaid these favors in French books, sending for example, works by Albert Camus after the writer's death in Algeria in 1960. That same year Devėnaitė wrote: "The travel document to Druskininkai, if you insist on paying for it, costs two tomes of the impressionists. I would very much like to have them!" (October 12, 1960, Šimaitė's Papers, Vilnius University). She arranged for a trial translation, a kind of literary audition, for Šimaitė's niece at the press in hope of securing her a decent job, but Aldutė first didn't show up, then failed the test on a second occasion. There was a falling out between Aldutė and Devėnaitė, and recriminations from Aldutė for Šimaitė's continued friendship and correspondence with her now-archenemy.

Of all Šimaitė's correspondents, Devėnaitė was the most deeply implicated in the Communist Party system; she was its biggest

23. Tayda Devėnaitė with her husband shortly before her suicide. Vilnius
University Library Rare Books and Manuscripts Department.

champion and believer. With regard to gender equality and femi-
nism in the USSR, according to the editor, all was well. Women
were now equals. She wrote to Šimaitė that her own path would
have been impossible in interwar Lithuania and credited her professional success to the Soviet system that, in her view, blind to
both gender and class, allowed a working-class girl to overcome
her origins. As for official atheism, this freed her from the time-
wasting rituals of Catholicism.

OCTOBER 20, 1960
Dear Ms. Ona! . . .
*I would now like . . . to disagree with your views on religion, censorship, and
so on. I hope you won't be angry if I actively lay out my thoughts on these
questions, which will not always agree with yours. . . .*
*First of all, with regard to religion and J. Ragauskas's book. From what
you've written, it's clear that being so far from your homeland, you don't
understand its conditions or the fact that for a long time religion spread
darkness over our people. It's not for nothing that our writers — from before
Žemaitė until now — have been writing on anti-religious themes. And that*

188

beautiful legend of Christ, that people themselves created, is exploited by the clergy to selfish ends. And what did religion do to woman? — it made her a slave. I am proud that I don't believe in God, even though I was baptized in the Catholic Church, and even though my conscious atheism didn't come easily. But now that I no longer attend church, I no longer pray, or rattle the rosary, I have much more time for useful work, good books, and travels. And I am even a great deal more independent and stronger now that I don't believe.

You should definitely come back to your homeland so that religious issues here would become clearer to you.

We have freedom of religion. My mother is religious, she goes to church, prays for all those godless children, and no one blames her for doing so — neither society, nor her family. But is it not painful to see a young person wasting time kneeling before an altar? I completely agree with the Soviet system and its anti-religious propaganda. In the future I will send you more anti-religious books about the clergy's business dealings. Let the facts speak for themselves if you doubt the honesty of my letter.

Of course, this is a very broad question, and I've laid it out very primitively. When we meet I will explain more fully (I still hope to meet you in Vilnius).

It's a similar situation with censorship. . . . We are consciously building a communist society and we must fight conscientiously, hard, and with intelligence for every person. Would it be better for our youth to have access to American comic books and French fashion magazines with half-naked women? Will we succeed like that? Is that what we call "individual freedom"? Is it not better that our youth read Chekhov and Gorky, that it have access to wonderful texts by Goethe, Maupassant, and even translations of Classical texts into our native language? Is this kind of literature not . . . worth fighting for? (Šimaitė Papers, Vilnius University)

How Šimaitė responded to this letter, I do not know. I have none of her letters to Devėnaitė, so I can only guess. We know that, above all, Šimaitė valued understanding, open-mindedness, and respect for the beliefs of others. Though an atheist, she loved scripture, sacred spaces, and the rituals that order religion. In response to a harsh critique of religious belief that her librarian friend Čilvinaitė (whom Šimaitė had sent in search of hidden Vilna Ghetto documents) published in a Lithuanian newspaper, Šimaitė wrote, "Get this one thing through that thick skull of yours: if you want others to respect your beliefs, then you must respect theirs in turn" (June 12, 1961, Šimaitė's Papers, Vilnius University).

Besides the book exchange, the need for medicine, and concerns for Aldutė, another major theme of the Šimaitė-Devėnaitė correspondence was the possibility of Šimaitė writing a memoir. Of all her friends and colleagues, Devėnaitė pushed her the hardest to write. When Šimaitė resisted Devėnaitė's every pressure tactic, the editor enlisted Čilvinaitė's help, but to no avail. "I don't know what to tell you about Ona Šimaitė's memoirs, wrote Čilvinaitė,

because she hasn't sent them to me, even though I've asked her time and time again to write them and send them, or to write them piecemeal in letters, but she hasn't done this either. We could ask her together, maybe that way we could succeed in getting something from her, since she knows . . . so much about the German occupation, the Vilna Ghetto and other places. (Letter to Devėnaitė, November 22, 1960, Čilvinaitė's Papers, Mažvydas)

Even in her final letters from the last year of her life, Devėnaitė continues to try to extract a memoir from her far-away friend, resorting to hypothetical threats:

As for your not wanting to write a memoir about the ghetto — if I could only reach you, I would surely beat you. . . . You have such rich material and show so much talent when you write about it (I read some pieces from your letters to Comrade Čilvinaitė, and I really liked them!). I will write to Dina [Abramowicz] and ask her to help by gathering any material you don't have. You may be angry or not, but I'll stick to my guns until the book comes out. . . .

The book about the ghetto must be finished! You can leave your memoir about Kazys Jakubėnas unfinished, you can stop answering letters altogether, and never attend another concert or play, but not to finish such an interesting book, when so much has been done already — this is not possible. I can see I'm starting to sound like a propagandist, so enough! Not one more word on the subject. . . .

In your life you've accomplished more than is possible or necessary. I know very little about you, but simply the fact that you helped Jews, the fact that you respond with such sensitivity to every request, whether for medicine, books, or something else, makes you a person respected by everyone — friends and strangers alike. What is most beautiful in my life is you and your gifts that arrive so frequently and selflessly. Thank you for being this way — kind, generous and forthright, when this is necessary. Thank you! (Illegible date, 1960, Šimaitė's Papers, Vilnius University).

When I have told North Americans about this correspondence and the enthusiasm of a 1960s editor for Šimaitė's memoir, the question that has arisen is: what's the catch? What's her angle? How did she want to distort Šimaitė's story to fit a Soviet narrative of the war? Was Devėnaitė interested in feeding a propaganda machine, or was her excitement genuine? Though she may have been naïve in her defense of a political and literary system that crushed dissent and censored creativity, from my readings of her letters, I believe her fervor was real.

Then, in 1961, something changed.

That year the editor's letters to Paris slowed down and eventually stopped altogether. In February 1961 Šimaitė wrote to Kauneckas, the Translator, asking him to phone the publishing house to check up on Devėnaitė from whom she had heard nothing since a minor falling out over books that the French postal service returned to Vilnius. Then, on April 27, 1967, Šimaitė wrote to Čilvinaitė: "She hasn't written to me since the New Year, and won't answer a single one of my questions. In November I sent her Anne Frank in German, but she hasn't yet let me know if she received it" (Šimaitė's Papers, Mažvydas).

Four months later Šimaitė finally received an update on Devėnaitė from Čilvinaitė. The news was not good. Devėnaitė had committed suicide in the summer of 1961:

After returning to Kaunas from my holidays I learned some sad news — Tayda died. She got married in the spring, lived with her husband for a month and a half then took her own life. I don't yet know the reason why; it's terribly sad and painful; I keep remembering her and can't believe that that lovely, talented and hardworking girl is no longer. As recently as last winter she asked for material about you and had some other writing plans; it seemed like she wanted to work, to live, and then suddenly it all fell apart.

Already a year ago something wasn't right. She always used to answer every query so quickly and cheerfully, then she changed somehow, her health started to fail and in the end, she broke off the life-thread. (Čilvinaitė's Papers, August 28, 1961, Mažvydas)

The death is mysterious and unexplained. No one knows why Devėnaitė chose to kill herself, and they are too discreet to tell Šimaitė how. Perhaps her reasons were personal, and something to do with her six-week-long marriage. Curiously, in none of her letters to Šimaitė does Devėnaitė mention a man in her life or a desire to marry. Quite the opposite: she revels in the power that she can wield as a woman in the USSR, and in the independence her job and salary afford her. We know that her closest friend, the poet Degutytė, lived openly as a lesbian. And Devėnaitė? Was her suicide perhaps a result of self-hatred or self-betrayal because of a negation of her sexual identity? Or were her reasons professional, and therefore political?

Given her position of influence, her youth, and travels, Devėnaitė must have been deeply implicated in the Party. Is it possible that at the age of thirty, she began to see and understand what she had been blind to before? Perhaps she somehow ended up on the wrong side of the authorities and was threatened in some way. Thomas Szasz writes that:

People kill themselves because they find life so unpleasant — so mentally or physically painful, so humiliating and hopeless — that dying seems to them more attractive than living. Biographers, novelists, playwrights, and poets have given us eloquent descriptions of the inner and outer circumstances of people who chose to die by suicide. As an abstract generalization we may say that the suicide is a person who feels trapped, often because he has suffered a grave defeat. (Szasz 59)

What was the defeat that Devėnaitė suffered? I have no answer to this question.

Like so many events in her past — events that Devėnaitė herself had pressured Šimaitė to write about — it seems that Devėnaitė's suicide is another occasion for silence. When I go to the diary that should contain entries from August, 1961, in search of what Šimaitė has to say about Devėnaitė's suicide, I discover a three-year gap. There is no diary for that time and therefore no reaction to Tayda's suicide — or rather, the reaction has perished. What happened to these three years? Did Šimaitė destroy these diaries? If so, why? Perhaps to protect herself or someone else? The Paris artist, Žibuntas Mikšys, who organized her papers after her death, wonders in writing on the first page of the diary if the missing notebooks have remained in the house of a family friend.

There are only two direct responses to Devėnaitė's suicide in Šimaitė's letters. On September 30, 1961 she wrote to the Translator:

Tayda's death was a real blow to me. There were no outward signs that she was suicidal. But during the year before her death, something had started to change in her soul. While a person is alive, often we don't understand them, and even wound them. But when we lose them, we see that these were just details, and that we had been incapable of noticing what was most important, the goodness, bigness and beauty of another's soul. (Kauneckas's Papers, Mažvydas)

And a month later, to Čilvinaitė:

I miss Tayda terribly. A person was alive, and you never think you could lose them. And then you regret not saying or doing all you could have. . . . (December 12, 1961, Čilvinaitė's Papers, Vilnius University)

It is her last mention of Devėnaitė.

It was not Šimaitė, but Devėnaitė herself who offered the most moving thoughts on the tragedy of a creative person's premature death. Referring to the death of the French actor, Gérard Philipe at the age of thirty-six, she wrote:

Deaths like his are the most painful. He would have done so much more, brought people so much joy, and then this! Why do people whom we need to live for millions of years, only get thirty-six years? Why can't we lend these people some of our years? Death always conceals some sort of cruel and sad secret, especially this kind. (November 27, 1959, Šimaitė's Papers, Vilnius University)

Devėnaitė was thirty years old when she killed herself.

By contrast, Janina Degutytė, the poet with the ailing heart, lived a long life. She died in 1990, a year before Lithuania restored its independence. I wonder in my more superstitious moments if Devėnaitė somehow ensured her friend's long life. In cutting her own life short, did she succeed in lending those unused years to her creative friend, with the caveat that she use the loan for writing? To be sure, Devėnaitė's death shrouds a terrible and cruel secret. We still don't know why she did it.

"Build your poems with my time," she might have told her friend. "It's the best I have to give."

CHAPTER 30

Paris 1968

THE city is up in arms. The songs that echo through the narrow
streets of the Latin Quarter littered with pamphlets remind Šimaitė
of her student days in revolutionary Moscow. But now Šimaitė feels
too old for revolution. She is no more than a spectator this time
around and can only lend silent support to the youth around her.
She is an aging revolutionary who lives life on paper, through letters,
and so for her, more significant than the marches and speeches, is
the French postal strike of May and June. The interruption in her
flow of letters is devastating. All ties to her family in Lithuania are
cut, and Šimaitė can only worry and wonder how Aldutė's mental
health is faring. So, in the absence of letters, and perhaps as a way
of exorcising her anxieties, she writes in her diary a short history
of Aldutė's troubles. Dated June 3, 1968, it's a sobering account and
includes details found in none of the letters. She appears to have
written it for posterity, for someone like me, who Šimaitė knew
or hoped would one day sift through her papers and come across
Aldutė's story. There's a sense here of her wanting to set the record
straight, to tell her niece's side for her since Aldutė's own version
of her life might garner little sympathy from a reader.

We already know of Aldutė's arrest at Šimaitė's apartment in
April 1944. But in the diary there is a story of a second arrest by
the NKVD. During the Stalin era — "the time of the cult" — Aldutė

studied classical piano at the Vilnius Conservatory and was good enough to perform in radio concerts. At the same time she began to study medicine, something she never enjoyed. And here, during her final year of studies: arrest and interrogation again. The story is a bit sketchy, and it's hard to decipher the exact reasons behind the arrest, but Šimaitė recounts that Aldutė lent a book to a friend whose sister was arrested shortly thereafter. When Aldutė appeared at her friend's home to retrieve the book, she too found herself taken into custody. She was in her early twenties when the secret police held and interrogated her for three weeks. There is no mention in Šimaitė's diary as to the reason behind Aldutė's arrest or that of her friend's sister. If the book was the cause, Šimaitė does not say so and perhaps doesn't know. It was, after all, a time when anyone could be arrested for anything. After her release from three weeks in custody, Aldutė was expelled from both the conservatory and medical school. She may indeed have been expelled because of her arrest, but there is another possibility. The diagnosis of schizophrenia may have been the reason for her expulsion, for such a diagnosis in the USSR had consequences:

The Soviet view of schizophrenia as an irreversible, deep seated illness with extremely broad diagnostic criteria leads to serious results for a large number of people who are labeled as suffering from it. They are liable, for example, to be deprived of their driving licenses, rejected for jobs, or barred from places in higher education. (Bloch and Reddaway 248)

A passage from Šimaitė's 1958 diary confirms the latter theory:

AUGUST 27, 1958
Of my two nieces, it was particularly difficult to write to the ill Aldutė. My advice was off the mark. Her cousin informed me in her letter that Aldutė suffered yet another great blow. Apparently, people who have been diagnosed with a mental illness are barred from the Faculty of Medicine. And without knowing this, I cruelly advised her to finish her last course and to study music later. Once I learned the truth, I had to comfort her immediately. And then I couldn't sleep for two nights. (Diary 21)

After the expulsion Aldutė suffered through six years of insomnia. She began to take medication to combat anxiety and aid sleep, and took on a physically demanding job at the botanical garden that didn't last. She was too weak and fragile. Her doctors recommended a change of atmosphere, a vacation if possible, since home life was becoming increasingly toxic for her. With Šimaitė's help via Devėnaitė, Julija succeeded in organizing a trip for her daughter to the mountains of the Caucasus. Marriage followed, then the birth of her son, an aborted second pregnancy, divorce, isolation, and her final descent.

24. Aldutė and Sasha. Vilnius University Library Rare Books and Manuscripts Department.

CHAPTER 31

Single and Crazy

THE spinster and the madwoman: each a stereotype of womanhood (for this is what women are: hysterical, mad, lonely), and, at the same time, not at all what women are supposed to be (self-effacing, nurturing, suppressing of their anger, selfless). While Šimaitė the spinster never expressed any desire in her letters or journals for marriage or an equivalent partnership with either men or women, Aldutė the madwoman lived in the hope that romantic love would save her. Šimaitė was an eternal self-sacrificing caregiver, while Aldutė in her aggression and anger, her neglect of self and of her child, was seen as dangerous and unwomanly. While Šimaitė was childless, Aldutė proved her womanhood by having her son. But in having her son, Aldutė broke definitively.

She met Sasha, an Uzbek sailor stationed on the Black Sea, on a train returning to Lithuania from the Caucasus. About ten years Aldutė's junior, Sasha had grown up in an orphanage, had few ties to his native Uzbekistan, and didn't think twice about moving to Vilnius to marry a woman he'd just met. The relationship worried Šimaitė, and rightly so, as it turned out. Apparently she was not alone in her apprehension:

DECEMBER 25, 1960
I'm sad. I've lit a pretty Swedish candle and submerged myself in memories of Christmas Eve in Lithuania with my loved ones. May they all be

well, especially Alduté. She made it through a challenging trip through the mountains, then met someone much younger than herself, whom she's fallen in love with. He's a sailor. Will she be happy? Or will new wounds open up? I'm so afraid for her. No one is talking openly about it, but everyone is nervous somehow. (Diary 24)

Sasha and Alduté's son was born in 1962, not quite a year after their wedding. The baby had "black hair and blue eyes. He weighed 2.9 kg, and was 50 cm long" (Aldona Stasionytė, June 23, 1962, Šimaitė's Papers, Vilnius University). A week later, Alduté wrote again, and all appeared to be well:

JULY 2, 1962

My Dearest, Beloved Onutė!
It's been a few days since I came home with my little one. They discharged him from the hospital even though the pediatrician said that he was still weak and didn't want to release him. But I feel fine. My only concern is for the little one. . . . In my opinion, he was a month premature, and should have been heavier by a kilo. . . . (Aldona Stasionytė, Šimaitė's Papers, Vilnius University)

But four months later, the situation had deteriorated significantly. Alduté's marriage was falling apart, and she blamed her family:

NOVEMBER 11, 1962

Hello My Dear Onelė!
I don't know if it's worth writing letters like the one I'm planning on writing here. They certainly won't bring you joy, which is already in such short supply, but perhaps it will make things easier for me. Perhaps you'll think that I'm abnormal, and will be of the same opinion as members of my family who "understand" me so well and know that I'm abnormal, and that one can only understand me and behave with me in the way proscribed by a psychiatrist (whom I've never consulted willingly).
It was a bit strange to read in your letter that my mother understands me so well. First of all, even though you may find it strange, and you may scold me, but in the depths of my soul, as long as I live, I will never call my mother "mother"! . . .
A long time ago you asked me if I was happy with Sasha. But you never

*asked me if I was happy with my family, or in the company of my relatives,
who "understand" me well, and even "love" me and want only "good" things
for me. . . . As for how much Sasha has helped me, this is only for me to know.
Whatever the truth may be, they were very thorough in filling Sasha in on
how abnormal I am, and how he should act with me. And so, I no longer
have what I so desired, and once again, I'm just a strange woman rather
than a wife or a friend, and for this I have my "do-gooders" to thank. . . .
My time is running out, even though I've only managed to write a few
fragments.*

*Perhaps you'll say that I'm writing in the midst of a psychotic episode, as
everything I do is explained away . . .[1] I don't care anymore. . .[2]*
Goodbye my childhood Sun!
Aldutė.
(Aldona Stasionytė, Šimaitė's Papers, Vilnius University)

From this point on, Aldutė's life begins to spiral out of control.
Her year of happiness with Sasha has come to an end, and the
marriage breaks down. The months following the birth of a baby
can be soul-crushingly difficult and lonely for women with loving
partners, well-functioning extended families, and relative financial
independence, so I would have been more surprised had Aldutė
come through psychologically and emotionally intact. Evidently, she
is not coping well and cannot put herself back on her feet, despite
attempts at buying herself time and space by hiring a caregiver
for the baby. Ultimately, it is Aldutė's son who bears the brunt of
the radiating tragedy of his mother's mental illness. At the age of
sixteen he stabs another youngster by a beer kiosk and serves two
years in jail.

My copies of Šimaitė's letters to Julija end in 1968. Šimaitė has
long been forbidden to write any more letters to Aldutė, and when
she tries to convince her sister that "a kind word carries a great deal
of meaning for a sick person as well," Julija won't be persuaded
(September 24, 1968, Šimaitė's Papers, Vilnius University). Aldutė
is now living on her own, raising her son, and has cut Sasha completely out of his son's life. Occasionally she shuts herself into her

apartment and won't let anyone in to see her. In her letters Šimaitė begs her sister not to commit Aldutė to a mental institution: "You mustn't take Aldutė to the hospital by force. Whose idea was this?" (September 24, 1968, Šimaitė's Papers, Vilnius University). In the end she prevails: "Julytė, I'm very thankful that you were able to take care of things so that Aldutė didn't have to be hospitalized" (November 24, 1968, Šimaitė's Papers, Vilnius University). With this letter the correspondence breaks off. Perhaps there were more letters that were destroyed, or perhaps the strain of Aldutė's health made further communication impossible. Little over eight months later, Šimaitė died. In her will she named the Paris artist, Mikšys, as the executor of her will. He went through her papers, bundled them in packages, labeled them in colorful inks and ex-libris plates, and sent them off to archives in the United States and Lithuania. Šimaitė's family members had the foresight to archive their letters as well.

More than twenty years after the bundling of those papers they found Aldutė one morning, frozen to death in her garden, wearing only a nightshirt. Kęstutis told me that it was either 1993 or 1994, but he wasn't sure anymore. Why she had gone out into the storm in the dark, no one could say. The door had evidently shut and locked behind her. She didn't go to the neighbors for help, perhaps because she was afraid of how they would receive her, the crazy lady. Aldutė, the schizophrenic. Perhaps she had gone outside in a state of confusion or in a fit. Or maybe it had been her intention to die, and she surrendered her battered body and soul to the elements so that they would deliver her of her pain.

PART NINE

CHAPTER 32

Cormeilles

ŠIMAITĖ spent her final years in an old age home that the Russian community established for its exiles in the suburb of Cormeilles-en-Parisis, located a short train trip from Paris. Though necessary, the move resulted in a near total loss of independence, and marked the beginning of a period of great unhappiness for Šimaitė. On March 1, 1966, she wrote in her diary:

I live in a building where 80 elderly people have been squeezed in. Many are 94–95 years of age. Among these six are insane. A good number are blind and deaf. . . . The atmosphere here weighs on me terribly. Everything is done according to a schedule. And I'm such an individualist, I can't stand living in these barracks. . . . If I could, I would abandon it all to live all alone once again in the worst conditions in Paris. (Diary 27)

Baby Sebastian accompanies me to the nursing home. After getting directions to the Zagor House from the local police station, we arrive as lunch is being served. A major complaint of Šimaitė's about life at Cormeilles was the poor quality of the meals: "Often I have to make do with bread . . . and tea or coffee — that's all," she wrote on February 28, 1969. "The food here is worse than in the prisons and camps" (Diary 29).

The doors are open, so we enter without difficulty and present ourselves at the main office. The director looks at me curiously when I explain why we have come, but arriving at an old age home with a baby is always a popular move, and Sebastian doesn't disappoint. This trip he is all smiles, and paves the way.

There is a commotion in the dining room, as the waitstaff eject a resident. *Il l'a fait exprès, je l'ai vu!* (He did it on purpose, I saw him!) cries a voice from around the corner. Monsieur Le Ciclé has a habit of breaking glasses at people's feet, and this time they have caught him in the act. Outside the dining room a woman cries in a nurse's arms. She wants a cigarette but isn't allowed to smoke until after the meal.

This kind of surveillance enraged Šimaitė. She, for one, ignored her doctor's orders and continued to prepare the fried fish and onion she loved on the hot plate in her room. Its aroma drifted down dark hallways and spread throughout the building, but Šimaitė would promptly eject unwelcome nurses and staff with a sharp word if they dared try curtail her freedom to eat and live as she saw fit. And she was not alone in her rage and despair. In addition to the shocking neglect of the Estonian woman, Šimaitė records the suicide of a neighboring resident:

JUNE 2, 1969

The last day of May was terrible. A good man hanged himself. Before dawn the police climbed in through the window (of the second floor) and took him away. He had shared a room with an insane person for three years. The atmosphere . . . of this place finally destroyed him. I bow my head to this hero, who ended his life, and had the courage to face such a difficult death as hanging. Today there was silence and sadness all around. (Diary 28)

By the next day, she later notes, staff and residents alike were speaking ill of the dead man.

More than anything, Šimaitė feared becoming a burden and being unable to care for herself. She read the experiences of those around her like cautionary tales and once wrote in her diary that she hoped to have the courage to take her own life if she ever reached a similar stage. Though her body had long ago begun to betray her, Šimaitė's mind remained sharp until the very end.

On January 17, 1970 the secretary of the Zagor House found
Šimaitė clinging to the wall outside her room. A letter from March
7, 1970 relayed the scene:

*She took Ona by the arm to help her to her room. But she was getting heavier
and heavier, so the secretary called for another staff member to help, and
take her by the other arm. But Ona fell to the ground. They called the nurse,
who gave her an injection to keep her heart beating, then she was taken to
her room on a stretcher. When the doctor arrived, he confirmed that Ona
had died. Her heart was exhausted. She was very heavy, and her heart too
weak. (Kauneckas, Šimaitė's Papers, Mažvydas)*

In accordance with her wishes, Šimaitė's body was donated to the
faculty of medicine in Paris. I have always considered this final act
both a generous gift and a heartbreaking display of self-abnegation.
Disdainful of waste and dismissive of worldly possessions and riches
as she was, Šimaitė's desire to be useful and instructive even after
death was entirely in keeping with her character.

But now, I wonder if there isn't more to it. Šimaitė has no grave.
I wonder if her rejection of burial was one more way of saying that,
to her, the body did not matter. To her, as a librarian, as an archivist,
and as a writer, what mattered most were the printed text and the
written word. Our bodies betray us all in the end. Bodies, unlike
brass buttons, do not endure and are therefore not worth burying,
not worth archiving. *Only what is written*, Šimaitė reminds us, *will
never die* (April 12, 1934, Kazys Boruta's Papers, Mažvydas). And
while I understand her and respect her ultimate gift, I see that things
are different for me and for Sebastian. For us, bodies do matter.
Mine gave me my son. The scars I have from the night of his birth
have given me a new way to write, whereas the scars Šimaitė had
from trials I will never know, silenced her.

Perhaps, on second thought, the body mattered to her more
than I realized.

CHAPTER 33

October

IT is autumn in Montreal. The leaves are turning for the first time in my son's life, and we take long walks to admire their colors. As we move under the rustling branches, I feel that we are not alone. Out of the corner of my eye I see the flash of a black hem disappear behind a tree. Moments later I catch a glimpse of a heavily stockinged ankle. He sees it too, I think, and he waves his arms and squeals in its direction. She is here, her presence unmistakable.

Notes

1. THE WOMAN IN THE PARK

1. Šimaitė copied the article into Diary 25 on July 18, 1964. The article, "Pagerbta lietuvaitė" (Lithuanian Woman Honored) comes from *Argentinos Lietuvis* (Argentinean Lithuanian), November 21, 1963.

3. CORRESPONDENCE

1. "Tautosaka" (Folktale) is Šimaitė's idiosyncratic term of endearment for Čilvinaitė, who had an interest in ethnography.

2. Unless otherwise indicated, ellipses are mine.

4. ONA ŠIMAITĖ'S LETTERS TO MARIJONA ČILVINAITĖ, 1957–1958

These letters come from Čilvinaitė's Papers at Mažvydas National Library. For an earlier English translation of the letters in this chapter, see Šimaitė "Letters from a Librarian."

1. Ellipses appear in the original.

5. CAREGIVING AND LETTERS

1. Ellipses appear in the original.

6. A CHILDHOOD TALE

1. In Lithuanian folklore, the devil (*velnias*) is a trickster, more mischievous than evil. In folktales devils may be outwitted.

7. RUSSIAN LETTERS

1. See Carolyn G. Heilbrun, Judy Long, and Elizabeth Hampsten, for example.

8. EVERYDAY WRITINGS

1. The French letters are archived at Vilnius University (Šimaitė's Papers), and the Russian at YIVO among Dina Abramowicz's Papers.

2. See Carol Ascher, Louise DeSalvo, and Sara Ruddick's excellent collection of essays, *Between Women*.

9. GHETTO

1. For an excellent textual tour of Vilnius and its history, see Laimonas Briedis's *Vilnius: City of Strangers*.

2. Ellipses appear in original.

10. MOWSZOWICZ

1. A specialist in the flora of the Vilnius region, Mowszowicz wrote his doctoral thesis and numerous articles about the plant life of Paneriai, whose forests would later become an execution ground. The son of a Vilnius barber, the botanist grew up in the shadow of the Gates of Dawn where he slept in a tiny windowless room. At the beginning of ghettoization, the University rector, Mykolas Biržiška, arranged for Mowszowicz to work in the city's botanical garden. The botanist later joined the ranks of the ghetto police, then of the sanitary police, who oversaw the ghetto's cleanliness. When he lost this position, Mowszowicz took it in stride, and devoted himself to teaching in the ghetto high school.

2. The poets Kazys Boruta and Kazys Jakubėnas are two examples.

11. LETTERS TO KAZYS JAKUBĖNAS, 1941–1943

These letters come from Kazys Jakubėnas's Papers at Mažvydas National Library. For an earlier English translation of them, see Šimaitė, "Letters from a Librarian."

1. Here, Šimaitė is most likely referring to Gershon Malakiewicz.

2. In the ghetto.

3. Kazys Boruta was a writer, best known for his work, *Baltaragio malūnas* (Whitehorn's Windmill).

4. Ellipses appear in original.

12. DESTRUCTION OF THE GHETTO

1. The name of the girl was Alė Berman. Šimaitė brought her to an orphanage under the name of Aldona Daujotaitė. Aldona was the name of both Šimaitė's nieces. Daujotaitė was her mother's maiden name. Šimaitė used

her niece Aldona Stasionytė's documents as the basis for the forged document. The Gestapo arrested Aldona at the same time as Šimaitė and interrogated her for a week.

13. KAZYS

1. Antanas Smetona was the president of Lithuania from April 4, 1919, to June 19, 1920, then again from December 19, 1926, to June 15, 1940, after deposing President Kazys Girnius in a *coup d'état*.
2. Pseudonyms included Maikis, Barabošius, P. Kalnietis, J. Sapalėlis, R. Bertašius.

16. CATHOLICISM, SEX, AND SIN

1. Ellipses appear in the original.

17. MOTHERING

1. Here I borrow Nancy Huston's image (714).
2. Tanya described being led out of the ghetto under a coat in her Hebrew testimony (Šimaitė, Righteous File).

19. FREEDOM

1. Ellipses appear in the original.
2. Ellipses appear in the original.
3. Ellipses appear in the original.

20. TOULOUSE

1. Ellipses appear in the original.

21. LETTERS TO NEW YORK

These letters are archived among Hirsz Abramowicz's Papers, YIVO.

1. This sentence appears in the original and is in Šimaitė's hand. Since she sent many of her promise-keeping letters through Jewish and other refugee organizations, this note was most certainly meant to ensure the letter reached the right Mr. Abramowicz.
2. Ellipses appear in the original.
3. Balys Norvaiša's unit carried out killings at Paneriai (Ponar).

23. THE GHETTO LIBRARY

I have based this chapter on Herman Kruk's diary published as *The Last Days of the Jerusalem of Lithuania*, on his essay "Library and Reading

211

Room in the Vilna Ghetto," and on Dina Abramowicz's "The Library in the Vilna Ghetto."

1. Ellipses appear in the original.

2. A religious text that sets out the order of the Passover Seder.

3. Shleyme-Zanvl Rapoport (1863–1920), "a native of Tshashnik (Čašniki, northeastern Belarus) who adopted the pseudonym An-ski (after his mother, Anna), is best known for his mystical play, *The Dybbuk*, first performed by the Vilna Troupe in 1920" (Katz 244).

24. LIBRARIANS

1. See Brugh and Beede, especially 943–47.

2. Genovaitė Raguotienė's book, *Greta įžymiojo Vaclovo Biržiškos*, offers fascinating portraits of the women surrounding Biržiška at the library, but even the title, which means "Beside the Influential Vaclovas Biržiška," confirms the women librarians' positions of metaphorical concubines.

29. DEATH IN VILNIUS

1. Devėnaitė writes that she can live on 500 rubles and that remaining 700, plus honoraria, are strictly for leisure. Compare this to Aldutė's situation that Kauneckas describes in a September 17, 1969, letter to Šimaitė: "Aldona is employed as a machine worker, and gets around sixty rubles. But her psychological state is getting worse, it's become impossible to have a conversation with her; she's harming her child; he's left unattended, unwashed, and maybe isn't being fed properly. So Julija has to go there constantly to try to help him. She says she can't see any way out" (Kauneckas, Šimaitė's *Correspondence*, Hoover).

31. SINGLE AND CRAZY

1. Ellipses appear in the original.

2. Ellipses appear in the original.

Works Cited

Abramowicz, Dina. "The Library in the Vilna Ghetto." *The Holocaust and the Book: Destruction and Preservation*. Ed. Jonathon Rose. Amherst: University of Massachusetts Press, 2001. 165–70.

———. "My Father's Life and Work." *Profiles of a Lost World*. By H. Abramowicz. Detroit: YIVO and Wayne State University Press, 1999. 18–35.

———. Personal Papers (Uncataloged). MSS and TSS. YIVO Archives, New York.

Abramowicz, Hirsz. Personal Papers. RG446, Correspondence with Anna (Ona) Šimaitė. MSS and TSS. YIVO Archives Archives, New York.

———. *Profiles of a Lost World: Memoirs of East European Jewish Life before World War II*. Trans. Eva Zeitlin Dobkin. Eds. Dina Abramowicz and Jeffrey Shandler. Intros. David E. Fishman and Dina Abramowicz. Detroit: YIVO and Wayne State University Press, 1999.

Ascher, Carol, Louise DeSalvo, and Sara Ruddick, eds. *Between Women: Biographers, Novelists, Critics, Teachers and Artists Write About Their Work on Women*. New York: Routledge, 1984.

Berger, Joseph. "Dina Abramowicz, 90, Librarian and Yiddish Expert, Dies." *New York Times* 9 Apr. 2000. Available online at http://www.nytimes.com. Consulted 17 Apr. 2009.

Bloch, Sidney, and Peter Reddaway. *Russia's Political Hospitals: The Abuse of Psychiatry in the Soviet Union*. London: Victor Gollancz, 1977.

Boruta, Kazys. Personal Papers. F10. MSS. Mažvydas National Library of Lithuania Rare Books and Manuscripts Department, Vilnius.

———. *Whitehorn's Windmill, or, The Unusual Events upon a Time in the Land of Paudruvė.* Trans. and Afterword Elizabeth Novickas. Budapest: Central European University Press, 2010.

Briedis, Laimonas. *Vilnius: City of Strangers.* Vilnius: Baltos Lankos and Central European University Press, 2009.

Brugh, Anne E., and Benjamin R. Beede. "American Librarianship." *Signs* 1.4 (1976): 943–55.

Chessler, Phyllis. *Women and Madness.* Garden City NY: Doubleday, 1972.

Čilvinaitė, Marijona. Personal Papers. F64. MSS. Mažvydas National Library of Lithuania Rare Books and Manuscripts Department, Vilnius.

Degutytė, Janina. *Poezija/Poems.* Trans. and ed. Mary G. Slavėnas. Vilnius: Lithuanian Writers' Union Publishers, 2003.

Duchen, Claire. *Women's Rights and Women's Lives in France, 1944–1968.* New York: Routledge, 1994.

Dworzhetsky, Marc (Meir). Personal Papers. P10/28, Correspondence with Anna (Ona) Šimaitė. Yad Vashem Archives, Jerusalem.

Felman, Shoshana, and Dori Laub. *Testimony: Crises of Witnessing in Literature, Psychoanalysis, and History.* New York: Routledge, 1992.

Freud, Sigmund. "Remembering, Repeating and Working-Through." *The Standard Edition of the Complete Psychological Works of Sigumund Freud.* Trans. James Strachey, vol. 12. Toronto: Clarke, Irwin, 1958: 152–53.

Friedlander, Judith. *Vilna on the Seine: Jewish Intellectuals in France since 1968.* New Haven: Yale University Press, 1990.

Gavelis, Ričardas. *Vilnius Poker.* Trans. Elizabeth Novickas. Rochester NY: Open Letter, University of Rochester Press, 2009.

Goldstein, Roberta Butterfield. *Cry Before Dawn.* Francestown NH: Golden Quill Press, 1974.

———. *Memories that Burn and Bless.* Francestown NH: Golden Quill Press, 1984.

Greenbaum, Masha. *The Jews of Lithuania: A History of a Remarkable Community 1316–1945.* Jerusalem: Gefen, 1995.

Hampsten, Elizabeth. *Read This Only to Yourself: The Private Writings of Midwestern Women, 1880–1910.* Bloomington: Indiana University Press, 1982.

Harshav, Benjamin. Introduction. *The Last Days of the Jerusalem of Lithuania.* By Herman Kruk. New Haven: Yale University Press and YIVO, 2002. xxi–lii.

Works Cited

Heilbrun, Carolyn G. *Women's Lives: The View from the Threshold*. Toronto: University of Toronto Press, 1999.

———. *Writing a Woman's Life*. New York: Norton, 1988.

Huston, Nancy. "Novels and Navels." *Critical Inquiry* 21.4 (1995): 708–21.

Jacobson, Dan. *Heshel's Kingdom*. Evanston IL: Northwestern University Press, 1999.

Jakubėnas, Alfonsas. "Kazio Jakubėno byla." Parts I and II. *Jaunimo gretos* November 1988: 21, 26–27; December 1988: 18–19.

Jakubėnas, Kazys. Personal Papers. F143. MSS. Mažvydas National Library of Lithuania Rare Books and Manuscripts Department, Vilnius.

Karvelis, Ugnė. "Un grand-duché multiculturel 1251–1772." *Lituanie juive 1918–1940: Message d'un monde englouti*). Ed. Yves Plasseraud and Henri Minczeles. Paris: Autrement, 1996. 34–53.

Kateiva, Jurgis. "Kas nužudė rašytoją K. Jakubėną?" *Naujienos* 30 Sept. 1958. No page numbers. Šimaitė's Papers. F244–117. Vilnius University Library.

Kauneckas, Vytautas. Personal Papers. F15–434. MSS. Mažvydas National Library of Lithuania Rare Books and Manuscripts Department, Vilnius.

Katz, Dovid. *Lithuanian Jewish Culture*. Vilnius: Baltos Lankos, 2004.

Kruk, Herman. *The Last Days of the Jerusalem of Lithuania: Chronicles from the Vilna Ghetto and the Camps, 1939–1944*. Ed. and intro. Benjamin Harshav. Trans. Barbara Harshav. New Haven: Yale University Press and YIVO, 2002.

———. "Library and Reading Room in the Vilna Ghetto, Strashun Street 6." Trans. Zachary M. Baker. *The Holocaust and the Book: Destruction and Preservation*. Ed. Jonathon Rose. Amherst: University of Massachusetts Press, 2001. 171–200.

Kundera, Milan. *The Book of Laughter and Forgetting*. Trans. Michael Henry Heim. New York: Knopf, 1980.

Long, Judy. *Telling Women's Lives: Subject, Narrator, Reader, Text*. New York: New York University Press, 1999.

Meras, Icchokas. Letters to Ona Šimaitė. 4691263. MSS (Photocopies). Yad Vashem Archives, Jerusalem.

Raguotienė, Genovaitė. *Greta įžymiojo Vaclovo Biržiškos*. Vilnius: Vilniaus Universiteto Leidykla, 2000.

Shoah. Dir. Claude Lanzmann. Videocassette, Paramount Home Video, 1986.

Šimaitė, Ona. Correspondence. Ona Šimaitė Collection. Box 1, folders

6 (Čilvinaitė) and 13 (Kauneckas). MSS and TSS. Hoover Institution Archives. Stanford University.

———. Diaries. F286–17. MSS. Vilnius University Library Rare Books and Manuscripts Department.

———. "Letters From a Librarian: Lost and Found in Vilna." Trans. and intro. Julija Šukys. *PMLA* 118 (2003): 302–17.

———. Personal Papers. F130. MSS. Mažvydas National Library of Lithuania Rare Books and Manuscripts Department, Vilnius.

———. Personal Papers. F286 (Šimaitė Collection) and F244 (Mikšys Collection). MSS. Vilnius University Rare Books and Manuscripts Department.

———. Righteous File 191. MSS and TSS. Yad Vashem Archives, Jerusalem.

Šimas, Kazys Kęstutis. *Ona Šimaitė — Pasaulio tautų teisuolė.* Vilnius: n.p., 2006.

Smith, Andrew Croydon. *Schizophrenia and Madness.* London: George Allen & Unwin, 1982.

Stankevičius, Rimantas. *Gyvenusi tautos himno dvasia.* Vilnius: n.p., 2004.

Steinberg, Isaac Nachman. *Australia, the Unpromised Land: In Search of a Home.* London: Victor Gollancz, 1948.

———. Personal Papers. 1023. MSS and TSS. YIVO Archives, New York.

———. *Spiridonova: Revolutionary Terrorist.* Trans. and ed. Gwenda David and Eric Mosbacher. Intro. Henry W. Nevinson. Freeport NY: Books for Libraries Press, 1971.

Šukys, Julija. *"And I burned with shame": The Testimony of Ona Šimaitė, Righteous Among the Nations." A Letter to Isaac N. Steinberg. Search and Research* 10. Ed. Dan Michman. Trans. of archival documents from Russian, with an intro. Jerusalem: Yad Vashem, 2007.

———. "Ona Šimaitė and the Vilnius Ghetto: An Unwritten Memoir." *Lituanus* 54.2 (2008):5–25.

Šuras, Grigorijus (Hiršas). *Užrašai: Vilniaus geto kronika 1941–1944.* Trans. Nijolė Kvaraciejūtė and Algimantas Antanavičius. Vilnius: ERA, 1997.

Szasz, Thomas. *Fatal Freedom: The Ethics and Politics of Suicide.* Syracuse NY: Syracuse University Press, 2002.

Tal, Merav and Shlomo. Personal interview. 10 Nov. 2003. Tel Aviv, Israel.

Urbšys, Juozas. Personal Papers. MSS. Mažvydas National Library Rare Books and Manuscripts Department, Vilnius.

Vatulescu, Cristina. "Arresting Biographies: The Secret Police File in the Soviet Union and Romania." *Comparative Literature* 56.3 (2004): 246–61.

Woolf, Virginia. *A Room of One's Own.* New York: Harcourt Brace & World, 1929.

———. *Women and Writing.* Ed. and intro. Michele Barret. New York: Harcourt Brace, 1979.